J... +
Happy ...
Great At

Καλώ ταχι...

WALKING IN WESTERN CRETE

45 WALKS IN KISSAMOS AND SELINOS

very best

Rosemary

...

Au...

The author on the western rim of Maganitra Gorge

About the Author

Alan Hall, a Scottish 'squatter' for 44 years, has written and photographically illustrated 10 outdoor and walking guides covering the Scottish Borders, the Lammermuirs, Kielder Forest, Northumberland, the north Pennines, North York Moors, Fife and Perthshire, and Lochaber – Ben Nevis and Glencoe.

An inquisitive pedestrian, full-time writer and photographer, Alan has walked in, in addition to Britain, Catalunya and the French Pyrenees, Italy and Sri Lanka, plus some 20 Greek islands and small areas on the Greek mainland. None more extensively, however, than his favourite, the addictive island of Crete.

Other Cicerone titles by the same author
Border Country – A Walker's Guide (3rd edition)
Walking in Northumberland (2nd edition)
Border Pubs and Inns – A Walker's Guide
Walks in the Lammermuirs – A Walker's Guide

pp : 120

KOOMAROS - shrub berry
used for 'RAKI'

WALKING IN WESTERN CRETE

45 WALKS IN KISSAMOS AND SELINOS

by

Alan Hall

CICERONE

2 POLICE SQUARE, MILNTHORPE, CUMBRIA LA7 7PY
www.cicerone.co.uk

© Alan Hall 2006
ISBN-10 185284 419 1
ISBN-13 978 185284 419 6

A catalogue record for this book is available from the British Library.
Photos by the author.

**Dedicated to Crete and Greta,
my inspirational partners**

Advice to Readers

Readers are advised that while every effort is taken by the author to ensure the accuracy of this guidebook, changes can occur which may affect the contents. A book of this nature with specific descriptions is more prone to change than some – waymarking can alter, for example, and new buildings go up or old ones disappear. It is advisable to check locally on transport, accommodation, shops, etc., but even rights of way can be altered and paths eradicated by landslip, forestry work or changes of ownership. The publisher would welcome notes of any such changes for future editions.

Front cover: A picturesque coastal section of the E4 south of Elafonisos (Walk 36)

CONTENTS

ACKNOWLEDGEMENTS

When you consider the frequency and ferocity of the many invaders of the fertile and intriguing island of Crete, throughout the centuries, BC and AD, it never ceases to amaze me how welcoming and helpful everyone has been in my search for a variety of walks that will please and stimulate. The response to my constant queries was always, 'You enjoy Crete to the full and return in years to come.'

I shall indeed return, to enjoy not only Kissamos and Selinos, but to be reunited with friends. To those who helped me, providing bed, food, directions, stories – fact and fiction – sights to see and ideas for what would make that particular walk unique, my sincere thanks. With no English, Christos and Anna Mapkakis and brother Stephano directed us from Afrata to the hidden shoreline cave of Ellinospilios. Thanks also to Kaliviani's Diktaki family, who introduced us to the heights and tales of Gramvousa Peninsula, the summits of Profitas Ilias and the secrets of Phalasarna. Our Katsomatados 'Panorama Taverna' mentors, the family of Manolis and Antonia Motakis, laid bare the entire landscape, history, folklore and gossip of Kissamos, as well as transporting us to and from several walks, and also introducing us to the Mayor of Kandanos. When the gods of Crete made Manolis they threw away the mould! In Vathi dwells Tassos Georgilas, supplier of local knowledge and a good friend, another to whom I am indebted, and also a first-class barber.

In the principality of Selinos little changed, the warmth of welcome and willingness to help remaining the same. In Paleochora Alekos Orfanidi, a man from Samos, via Australia, and his wife Rena, had much to tell about Paleochora and surrounds, plus a large, fast car that took me in style to the start of several walks, including Kandanos, 'capital' city of Selinos, to meet once again Constantinos Kontados – Mayor of Kandanos. On learning of my intentions the Mayor said, 'Your interest in our area made us all very glad – when you come, we'll all help you, because your work may help us to bring out our sightseeing.' I am also greatly indebted to Eleni Kalogridi, the Mayor's English-speaking PA and my guiding light for this treasure trove of walks from Kandanos.

In Kandanos we had great fun, much happiness and fine meals, while learning the secrets of the old ways from Soula Mathewdaki, born in the mountain village of Spina, who in childhood walked through the 'Spinatiko' – Spina Gorge – to Kandanos High School. Who better to advise me concerning Kandanos to Spina? Next was Angela Miridakis, whose parents originated from Kandanos and emigrated to Australia, where Angela was born and raised. After university this firecracker visited Kandanos, stayed and married. Now she helps run the coffee shop and café bar. Samantha Ntountoulakis, whose family have the taverna at the corner of the town square, also opened up the surrounding mountains and hills for us. What better venues from which to gain local knowledge?

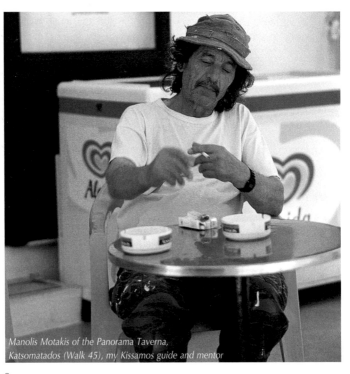

Manolis Motakis of the Panorama Taverna, Katsomatados (Walk 45), my Kissamos guide and mentor

Crete

Area covered in this book

Kastelli
Chania
Kandanos
Paleochora
Rethymnon
Heraklion
Zakros

N

0   12   24 km

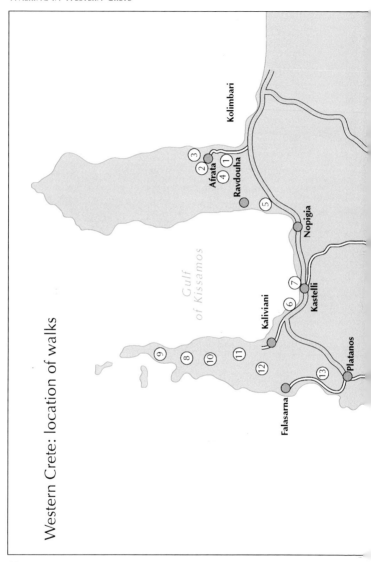

Western Crete: location of walks

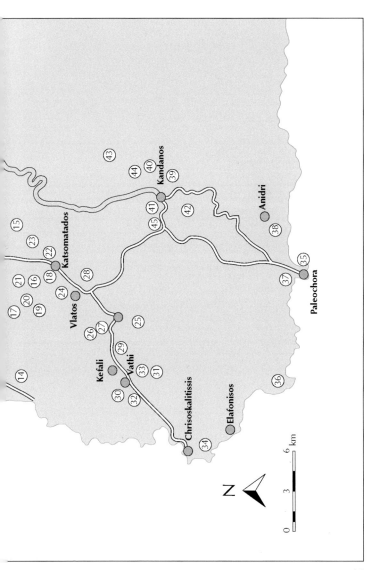

Map Key

══════	major road
───────	country road
▬▬▬▬	dirt track
··············	route
▬▬▬▬	tarmac road
‑‑‑‑‑‑‑‑	footpath
⌁	river/water
◉	town
■	habitation
Ⓢ	start of walk
▲	summit
✝ ●	church/chapel
✦	monument
▣	ruin/antiquity
©	cave
Ⓜ	museum
▒	sand
P	parking
⌸	castle
⸮⸮⸮⸮⸮	gorge
⏥	port
⚘	fountain
⸸	communication mast

INTRODUCTION

*To paraphrase Nikos Kazantzakis, from Report to Greco,
'The soul of Crete has blossomed within me'.*

KISSAMOS AND SELINOS

Grecophile or not, few places in the world can stir the soul or quicken the heartbeat more than the hazy outline of Crete, when seen from either sky or sea. The largest island of this country of islands rises phoenix-like between the blue waters of the Cretan Sea and the Libyan Sea. It matters not whether the plane or the ferry lands or docks at Chania or Heraklion, emotions are the same, although cosmopolitan, historical Chania is our preferred point of arrival for Western Crete, pleasing on the eye and with the stamp of many influences. Its main attraction is that it provides swift passage of one and a half hours or so, via a good bus service, to the intriguing western extremities of Kissamos and Selinos.

This richly varied landscape, 50% classed as mountainous and 17% as fertile cultivated land, covers approximately 900 sq km (347 sq miles). Central Agios Dikeos above Elos, at 1184m (3885ft), is the highest mountain within Kissamos, and Agios Zinon above Spina, at 1333m (4374ft), the giant of Selinos. There are gorges aplenty, including Sirikari, Halasses/Portopharaga, Maganistra,

Cloud-crowned Rodopou Peninsula over the Gulf of Kissamos (Walk 10)

Over the Gulf of Kastelli to the Lefka Ori (White Mountains) (Walk 10)

Keramariano, Anidri, Spina and Topolia, the latter now unfortunately closed by extensive rock falls (2003–2004). Two spectacular peninsulas, Rodopou and Gramvousa, have fertile plains and plateaux clad with 'the golden tree' (the olive), known in bygone days as 'the divine tree'. Olive trees cover 70% of cultivated land within Western Crete, and it is doubtful if any walks in this guide are entirely olive-tree free.

Ridge after ridge of challenging heights and summits provide grandstands, far-seeing views and sightings beyond compare. Each village, church or chapel, river or lake, town or harbour, trail or track, shoreline or sand dune, mountain ridge or rocky summit has a story to tell for the adventurous and inquisitive.

Populated by a proud and honourable ancient race, rich in history and hospitality, this colourful canvas of silvery olives is framed by golden sand, shimmering lagoons and towering cliffs. It is a bountiful, fertile patchwork of vineyards, olive groves and white villages. The area invites exploration by those with an inquisitiveness about and appetite for ancient civilisations and new horizons.

This paradise lies west of a line wriggling south for 50 tortuous kilometres (31 miles) from Tavronitis, overlooking the western extremities of the Bay of Chania, via the restored municipality of Kandanos in the Selinos district, to the coastal peninsula of Paleochora. Surrounded by the Libyan Sea and sandy beaches, this popular expanding 'township' is overlooked by the countless olive groves that enhance the adjoining lower slopes of mountainous Sfakia.

The remaining boundaries are within the northern coastline, which includes the charismatic peninsulas of

Rodopou and Gramvousa framing the Gulf of Kissamos. The eye-catching western seaboard comprises extensive sandy beaches, stark rock cliffs and the unique lagoons of Balos and Elafonisos, situated on the island's northwest and southwest extremities. The package is finally and securely enclosed by a southern coastline of low, rounded hills, sandy bays and, finally, west of Paleochora, a tomato hamlet of plastic *thermokypra* (greenhouses).

The area contains three small, but in recent years expanding, townships: Kastelli, the commercial centre and small port within the Gulf of Kissamos; Kandanos, a municipality that grew phoenix-like from the ashes of war into today's capital of the principality of Selinos; and thirdly picturesque Paleochora, astride its narrow peninsula overlooking the Libyan Sea, and crowned with a crumbling Venetian fort.

The variations of terrain, history and interest within the provinces of Kissamos and Selinos and surrounds constantly challenge and delight. On offer are a selection of mountain treks, ridge and hill walks (which include sections of the waymarked E4 – European Long Distance Trail), gorge explorations, cliff and coastal walks, village-to-village rambles, olive-grove and sweet-chestnut strolls (Elos is Crete's sweet-chestnut centre), or simply the opportunity to prowl around the many archaeological wonders. These include the ancient Dorian city of Polyrinia, the sunken pre-Hellenic naval harbour, also Dorian, at Falasarna/Phalasarna (where the finest Myzithra cheese in Crete is made), or the Mycenaean and Roman ruins at Kastelli. Also of interest are the Byzantine churches and their wall paintings within Selinos, and to a lesser extent at Kissamos.

WALKING IN WESTERN CRETE

For convenience I have included several contrasting walks from a selected base (where varied accommodation is available), moving to the next base by bus or taxi, or perhaps with a linear walk. This enables the area to be explored if the walker does not have transport. Suggested bases are **Kolimbari**, **Afrata**, **Ravdouha**, **Nopigia**, **Kastelli**, **Kaliviani**, **Falasarna**, **Platanos**, **Katsomatados**, **Elos**, **Kefali**, **Elafonisos**, **Paleochora**, and **Kandanos**.

Walking in Crete can be dehydrating. Ensure that you and your water bottle are topped up daily, a minimum of 5 litres and 2 litres respectively. Apricots, fresh or dried, should also be taken, the fruit for energy, the stones to suck to keep your mouth moist. Springs are often met along the way, and if I am sure they are clean and safe to drink from, they are mentioned in the route descriptions. Those which are not should be treated with caution.

Another minus, albeit minor, is the infrequency of waymarks along the way, but regard this as a challenge.

15

UK-style mountain rescue services are unavailable in the area covered by this guide. My advice is: 1) make a note of the telephone number of the nearest police station, and 2) leave details of your route and ETR with your host/landlord.

CLIMATE AND WEATHER PATTERNS

The clarity of Crete's air and the blue of its skies are renowned, Paleochora averaging only 44 cloudy days per year compared with 58 in Athens. Mythology recounts that Apollo, god of light and sun, was forever faithful to his beautiful nymph, who dwelt in southern Crete, never leaving even during winter months.

Crete stands high on the climatic table of Mediterranean sun, second only to Cyprus. Crete's sun shines for 300 days a year. Remember, the south coast and flat, sheltered lands are hotter than the north coast or the high mountains.

November marks a dramatic change, with the onset of rain, heavy at times, and in mountainous areas rapid falls in temperature. Frosts and snow are seldom seen on the coasts, particularly the south coast. There is, however, the exception, as happened in January 2004 over Paleochora, whose average December–January temperature is 16°C and on whose immediate mountainous hinterland the snowline lies at approximately 610m (2000ft). A heavy blanket of snow, the first and only one in living memory, brought the snowline down to sea level, covering this sun-blessed resort in several inches of this strange

Western Crete: Climate

Month	Temp	Hours of Sunshine	Days of Rain
January	14°	157	13
February	13°	160	10
March	14°	210	8
April	17°	244	4
May	19°	303	3
June	24°	359	1
July	27°	388	0
August	28°	367	0
September	26°	302	2
October	22°	248	5
November	19°	181	8
December	18°	152	12

Average temperature (°C), sunshine and rainy days per month

white substance, and bringing the town to a complete standstill.

Crete, as with most islands, particularly those bounded with a large landmass beyond their surrounding seas, is influenced by the prevailing winds. The south coast escapes the rigours of the northwesterly *meltemi*, but not the dust storms of the tempestuous *sirocco,* a wind that blows, hurricane force at times, into the south coast via the Libyan Sea from Libya (where it is called *livas*). This southerly wind carries fine particles of yellow/red dust from the Sahara, depositing its load into every nook and cranny. Simultaneously the atmosphere becomes close, hot, heavy, silent and eerie. It can also reach the northwest extremities of the island. All Crete's disasters are attributed to this distasteful south wind, including the devastation of Knossos. I experienced the *sirocco* and its deposits once in my 12 visits to Crete – our hosts on the Gramvousa Peninsula required four sessions, with power-hose and brushes, to clean their veranda, tables and chairs.

At the end of a hot summer the *meltemi* brings a cool air flow from the Cretan Sea to Crete's north coast, mellowing the savage heat of high summer, although at times this initially pleasing wind increases in strength to 8–9 Beauforts, whipping up sandstorms on the island's beaches.

A third wind, the *punentis*, blows in the winter months from the west/southwest, bringing not hurricane strength nor Sahara dust, but a high percentage of Western Crete's seasonal rain.

The best months for walking are April (flowers in bloom), May, early June, September and October. July and August are inclined to be hot, dusty and parched, and are to be avoided should your intention be more than a shady stroll.

FLORA AND FAUNA

Flora

Crete as a whole, and the lower sheltered plateaux and wider valleys of Kissamos and Selinos in particular, are as productive and colourful as any Mediterranean 'Garden of Eden'. Herbs, small shrubs and flowers number around 1350 species, of which approximately 12% are indigenous to Crete.

Most likely to be met 'along the way' are **horta**, a spinach-like wild vegetable that when cooked is good to eat. Ankle-high **thyme**, **oregano**, **sage** and **marjoram** can be seen fringing cliffs and plateau paths, as well as the inedible tangle of **gorse**, **myrtle**, **juniper**, **convolvulus**, and the everpresent, wildwalker's nightmare, the prickly **phrygana**. This is found infesting dry, rocky ground, and is identified by its ground-hugging, 'domed', angled network of thorny branches that conceal ankle-turning rocks and stones – as we found to our cost when researching Walk 9 (Vouxa).

Beware also the sharp spines of **prickly pear** and the large, dark-purple – almost black – flowers of a lily that lurks in shady gullies and gorges, known as the 'stinking' or 'stinky' lily. Should you meet this malodorous member of a sweet-scented family, admire it from a distance. On the plus side are colourful red **poppies**, **tulips**, **cyclamen**, **peonies** and occasional **orchids** in gorges and gullies.

Cultivated plants include the **vine**, whose fruit is of prime importance to the Cretan economy, which, during centuries of abstemious Turkish Muslim domination, was almost wiped out. Fortunately, after the Turkish occupation ended, viticulture recovered, with vines now thriving at altitudes in excess of 914m (3000ft). Not only wine is produced, but grapes are also sun-dried to produce **sultanas**. It is estimated Crete nurtures some 50 million **olives**, its economic mainstay, plus **citrus fruits**, **apples**, **apricots**, **plums**, **peaches** and *moura*.

Climbing up the 'height' scale, the ever-present, prominent **aloe cactus** is instantly recognisable by its 2-metre-plus flowering stems. Also found is the distinctive, evergreen **carob tree**, whose aromatic black pods are harvested for paper manufacture, medicinal purposes (since ancient times) and animal feed. Many indigenous flora were used by Hippocratian physicians, for example **rue** (*Ruta chalepensis*) as a cure for

hysteria and an antidote for snake bites. **Thyme** and **sage** are aromatic, also possessing pharmaceutical qualities, and both are in demand by bees to produce the area's renowned honey. Surrounding Rodopou and Afrata is the much-sought-after **wild artichoke**.

In ancient times Crete was clothed with forests of **cedar** and **cypress**, but not so today. First came the Minoans, who felled great swathes for pillars for their palaces, but later it was plunder that decimated the woodlands. Both Venetians and Turks stripped the forests to build houses and ships, to produce charcoal, and to lay bare the land to remove the hideouts of Cretan resistance. These practices were also carried out by the Germans during their 1941–45 occupation of Crete. Evidence of tree regeneration can be seen above Vlatos (Walk 24) thanks to the replacement by post-war foresters from Germany. Today preservation and regeneration throughout the area has produced pockets of thriving **cypress**, **platania** (plane tree) and **castanea** (sweet chestnut) (Walks 22, 23 and 25). Elos, surrounded by the largest chestnut groves, is the main supplier of sweet chestnuts in Crete. Many platania trees stand tall and leafy alongside watercourses, indicators of a constant supply of water. **Tamarisk**, a thin, waif-like tree, seen on beaches and promenades, has a unique characteristic in the form of special glands that enable it to excrete

Afrata – village of flowers (Walk 2)

salt. What better place to examine this unique phenomenon than by the beach and promenades of Paleochora (Walk 35). Note **eucalyptus** – strong trunk, thick foliage and a bark that tends to fall off in strips – also a sign of plentiful water.

Fauna

There are no poisonous snakes in Kissamos or Selinos, or for that matter in all of Crete – legend states that Agios (Saint) Titos banished them for all time! There are however millions of noisy **cicadas** (cricket family) that croak constantly, although this is only the males, prompting a learned man from ancient times to utter, 'Blessed are the cicadas, for their females are silent'! Probably as a result of their energy-sapping vibrations, they die in September, and the quiet in October is almost deafening!

The largest wild animal is the Cretan **wild goat** (*kri-kri*), but its numbers are dwindling, and it is seldom seen, as it grazes at night and hides during the day. Do not confuse this impressive animal, with its huge curving horns, with the domestic goat seen at every corner. Other small animals are **hares** and **rabbits**, as well as **domestic sheep**, **mules**, **donkeys**, **cats** and **dogs**. The dogs seem to live permanently on the end of chains attached to the property of their masters, and hurl themselves, snarling and slavering, at any approaching pedestrian. I met two such guardians on a fenced track before an ascent of

Manna (Walk 14). As I approached they hurled themselves into the middle of the dusty lane, leaving a gap of 15–23cm (6–9in). Sweet-talking the 'good doggies' allowed me unmolested passage – they wagged their tails, scampered back to their posts and sat down.

Last but not least is the **mosquito**, a biting gnat that is the scourge of mankind and which concentrates at low levels, particularly in areas where there is exposed water. I found from experience that the higher you climb the fewer mosquitoes you meet. Always have mosquito repellent to hand and make sure it contains 'diet' (*diethyltoluamide*).

The bird population within the island can be found around the coastline, in gorges, alongside rivers, in forests of pine or broadleaves, or on mountains above 1800m (5905ft). Western Crete, particularly Kissamos and Selinos, lies directly south of the Peloponnese on one of the major migratory routes between mainland Europe and North Africa. The two prominent peninsulas of Rodopou and Gramvousa are of great importance for migratory birds to and from Europe. Forty-seven species of birds, 19 of them migratory, nest on and around the two peninsulas and the habitats of Kissamos and Selinos, including Elafonisos.

Large raptors – **vultures** and **eagles** – are the most conspicuous. They are seen at their best in mountainous areas above 610m (2000ft), together with **buzzards** and **crows**, while in the valleys and gorges and around the coast are found **shrikes**, **warblers**, **finches**, **larks**, **swallows**, **swifts**, the occasional **nightingale** (at Katsomatados), and coastal seabirds such as several species of **gull**.

Significant events affecting Kissamos and Selinos are given below.

Neolithic, 6000BC–2600BC (New Stone Age). Crete's first inhabitants came from either Asia Minor or the northern fringes of Africa, although others theorised that these 'incomers' did encounter indigenous peoples who initially existed as hunter-gatherers living a semi-nomadic existence, advancing through crude agricultural practices and tools to fashion copper, stones and clay. As 2600BC approached numbers of peoples from areas now known as Turkey, Egypt and Libya, and other Greek islands, settled in Crete.

Bronze/Minoan Era, 2600BC–1100BC. These civilised settlers combined with the indigenous peoples to collectively become 'Minoans', and for the next 1400 years they developed Crete into an advanced civilisation. Unfortunately they left no written records. This 'Minoans' period is divided into four:

Pre Palatial, 2600BC–2000BC During this period innovative techniques were introduced that increased general knowledge and developed the Minoan arts, e.g. the potter's wheel, ceramic colours and styles. Overseas trade grew, as did agricultural skills and the construction of permanent dwellings.

Old Palatial, 2000BC–1700BC. Sculpture, jewellery and ceramics, e.g. the 'eggshell ceramics' found in the Kamares Cave in the Ida Mountains of central Crete, developed. Of greater significance was the emergence of primitive hieroglyphics, a numerical technique. An expanding and commercially successful import/export trade produced a 'hierarchial' (government by priesthood) civilisation. The fateful earthquake of 1700BC eradicated visible signs of success, ending the era of Old Palatial.

New Palatial, 1700BC–1400BC. Minoan society reached its zenith, imports/exports flourished and Crete controlled the Mediterranean Sea. South of Heraklion stood the capital, Knossos, with Minos as monarch, his throne reputed to be the oldest in existence in Europe. Women were respected and conspicuous (note the surviving frescoes and statuettes). Again disaster struck in 1400BC, destroying Crete's palaces and

Ancient Polyrinia and the Church of 99 Saints (Walk 17)

major buildings. A volcanic eruption of unimaginable force on the island of Thira (today's Santorini), 121km (75 miles) north of Crete, created a huge tsunami that overwhelmed the entire island.

Post Palatial, 1400BC–1100BC. With the Minoan influence in tatters, the Mycenaeans had increasingly infiltrated, and by now they controlled Crete.

Dorian Period, 1100BC–500BC. The Dorians from Hellenic Greece, armed with superior iron weapons, overran the mainland Mycenaeans, and continuing south to Crete, overpowered the island, an invasion that ended Crete's 'Golden Days'. Broken into many pieces, each governed by a 'township', internal bickering led to

international insignificance. Sparta and Athens now fashioned Greek history, moulding Crete into an island of discontent, home to pirates and brigands.

Roman Period, 67BC–395AD. The integration into the Roman Empire was long and painful. It was two years before Roman General Metellus delivered the fractious child, Crete. The advantages of Roman occupation were a cessation of inter-city conflicts, a network of Roman roads crisscrossing Crete and the introduction of Christianity. In 395AD the declining Roman Empire was divided into the Eastern and Western Roman Empires, with Crete now governed from Byzantium – the old name of Turkey's capital Istanbul (also known as Constantinople from 330AD to 1926).

Byzantine Crete, 395AD–651AD. A period of Christianity (the Eastern or Greek Church) when many churches were constructed. It was also a time of expansion by the followers of Islam beyond Crete.

Turkish Arab Domination. The Arabs came twice to Crete in the Byzantine period – 651–674AD and 823–961AD, – disrupting the spread of Christianity and destroying many Byzantine churches. After several attempts Cretan forces recaptured Crete, laying the foundations for the second Byzantine era.

Second Byzantine Period, 961AD–1204. Many Christians returned from Asia Minor to bolster the depleted population. It was also a period of division within the church, segregated into Orthodox and Roman beliefs. The Cretans accepted the Orthodox creed.

The Venetians, 1204–1669. Conflict continued during the Crusades, when a coalition from Western Europe destroyed Constantinople. The Republic of Venice bought Crete from the Crusaders for 'a widow's mite'. Cities were developed while the countryside was brought to its knees by excessive taxes, resulting in at least 10 revolutions exploding in the first 150 years. The 15th century brought fresh problems. Constantinople is recaptured by the Turks, forcing the Venetians to build fortresses throughout Crete using Cretan slaves (see Imeri Gramvousa,

Walks 8 and 9). With the Turks' return in 1669, its economy in tatters, Crete was once again under the yolk of Islam.

Turkish Occupation, 1669–1898. The Turks bled Crete dry. Increasing taxes, decimating forests, cities and harbours, they attempted to convert every Cretan, by force, to Islam. Driven into the mountain ranges of Western Crete, the Cretans regrouped, and in 1770 rose in revolt under Yannis Vlachos, 'Daskaloyannis' – 'John the Teacher'. Disastrously, the Turks lured John the Teacher to Heraklion for peace discussions, where they captured him and, in front of his brother, skinned him alive. Many monuments to his memory remain. In 1821 Crete revolted again, joining Greece against the Turks, and in 1832 Greece declared its independence from Turkey. Unfortunately, European powers ceded Crete to Egypt, which in 1841 allowed the Turks to return, although in 1898 the combined powers of Europe forced the Turks out.

Self-governing Crete, 1898–1913. Crete's High Commissioner was the younger son of the Greek King, Prince George. He retired when Cretan Eleftherios Venizelos became Prime Minister of all Greece in 1910.

Union with Greece, 1913–41. Greece signed a treaty with Turkey on 30 May 1913, formally assigning Crete to Greece.

German Invasion, 1941–45. On 21 May 1941 German troops came out of the sky at Maleme, lighting a fuse that eventually killed 5000 Greeks, 1527 Allied forces and 4465 Germans.

ACCESS

Air links provide the first stage from Britain for the journey to Chania, Western Crete. Three possible options, at the time of publication, are available.

1) A choice of airlines or train services to London's Heathrow or Gatwick airports for scheduled air services to Athens, with connecting services, e.g. Olympic or Aegeon, to Chania.

2) 'Cheap and cheerful' airlines to Athens, e.g. EasyJet from London's Gatwick or Luton airports.

3) Charter flights offer some 'flight only' seats, as opposed to package holidays, flying from London airports and larger provincial airports direct to Chania.

Ferryboat Connections Should you wish to vary your mode of transport to/from Athens to Chania, there are fast ferryboats operating to/from Piraeus/Souda Bay to Chania. Departing nightly at 20.00hrs, they arrive the following morning, **but please check details**. The Piraeus departure dock is some 10 minutes' walk from Piraeus metro station; Souda Bay dock is 3–5 minutes' walk. Tickets are available from harbourside agents or the ship's gangway desk, and vary in price. (At the time of writing – 2004 – it was £25 (35 euros) return.) Improved facilities are more expensive.

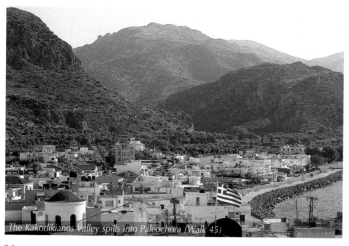

The Kakodikianos Valley spills into Paleochora (Walk 45)

A floral ascent to Leventies' summit (Walk 22)

Local Taxi Services As in most places there are good and not so good, although I have found the country taxi service to be reasonable and most helpful. The majority of accommodations will gladly arrange for a local taxi as required, and if walking along a roadside after a hard day, a raised hand or a whistle will stop any passing taxi.

Local Bus Services Your first encounter with the local buses will most likely be KTEL network bus station in central Chania, from where a good service operates regularly into the regions of Kissamos and Selinos. Relevant timetables, changed each May, are available at Chania, Kastelli and Paleochora. There is a left luggage facility in Chania, open from 07.00hrs–20.00hrs. Bus tickets are bought from the station or on the bus, with departures in Greek and English announced or on display at the ticket desk. Sizeable luggage should be placed in the hold and the driver/conductor told of your destination.

Buses to the starting points of many of the walks go to and pass by: Kolimbari, Nopigia, Kastelli, Topolia, Katsomatados, Elos, Vathi, Monastery Chrisoskalitissis and Elafonisos; also Tavronitis, Kandanos, Kakodiki, Spaniakos and Paleochora. Buses from Kastelli also go to Kaliviani, Platanos and Falasarna. Some school buses provide passage to walk starts and from finishing points, details of which are included, if relevant, in the appropriate walk description.

On Foot Kissamos and Selinos provide infinite varied *stremas* (1000 sq m) of scenic excellence and kilometres of donkey trails, dirt tracks and paths, public pathways and quiet roads. Many utilise yesterday's roads – trade routes, drove roads, carrier's ways and paths from village to church and church to farm. Where the landowner does not wish us to walk, the way is invariably bolted and barred. Respect their wishes and do not tamper with locked or secured gates.

As many walks inspect the tiny Byzantine churches met along the way, please ensure that these holy places are respected, and that when leaving, doors are securely closed. Considerate walkers will appreciate that the majority of walks in this guide are on public paths, byways, permissive paths, donkey trails, church paths and old trade routes, although these are not shown as such on the non-too-informative small-scale sketch maps in the guide. These ways should be adhered to – **use the routes as illustrated within this guide**. The majority of walk routes have been given to me by knowledgeable and responsible local people whose ancestors have walked these ways for generations. Every walk is the result of in-depth conversations and discussions with local walkers, farmers, landowners, walks guides, hoteliers, taverna landlords, historians, ex-sevicemen, the Mayor of Kandanos and his PA Eleni, plus my mentor and guide – the fountain of Katsomatados tales and folklore – Manolis Motakis of the Panorama Taverna.

ACCOMMODATION

A variety of accommodation, at the moment approximately half the UK price, can be found throughout Western Crete, ranging from large hotels (invariably in the main towns such as Kolimbari, Kastelli, Falasarna and Paleochora) and of course in Chania, the gateway to Western Crete.

Small hotels and apartments are available also at Kaliviani, Platanos, Elos and Elafonisos. By far the most prevalent and in many cases the most popular economic accommodation is in rooms, many attached to tavernas, throughout Kissamos and to a lesser extent Selinos. Room rates (which vary throughout the season) are set annually by the Tourist Board and displayed in each room, showing the maximum price that can be charged.

The location of approved accommodation is given in Tourist Board booklets available from their offices, and also some bookshops and newspaper shops. Tavernas and rooms invariably display prominent notices advertising their services, although perhaps the best information is obtained by asking at the local taverna or bar.

Most walks in this guide have been selected, where possible, in clusters that surround or are in close proximity to suitable accommodation, with transport links to the start/finish, and not too far away from the next cluster of walks. I found when researching the walks that our hosts would willingly book our next base for us.

USING THIS GUIDE

Spelling
Place names, when translated from Greek to English, often have two or three different spellings, depending on which book/map you are reading.

Although the place name may look different, the English pronunciation is invariably the same, e.g. the Monasterie 'Chrisoskalitissis/ Chrysoskalitissa', or 'Polirrinia/ Polyrinia'. To avoid confusion I have endeavoured to present the most frequently used English spelling.

Aim

My aim has been to produce a walks guide that enables the reader and the walker to enjoy the delights and surprises of Selinos and Kissamos; a book that conveys my enthusiasm for this relatively unknown, but incomparably diverse Greek Island. The 45 walks sample Western Crete's scenic strengths and man's achievements, as found in its cities, townships, villages, ancient holy places, coastlines, peninsulas, gorges, high plateaux and mountain ranges, providing a mix to suit pedestrians of all interests and abilities.

Maps

Unlike British OS Landranger and Explorer maps and French Carte de Randonnée maps, the Greek maps are but blunt tools and should only be used as indicators of the broad picture, with the book's sketch maps and route descriptions providing finer details, such as compass bearings, for the walker. The maps below are the most up to date and accurate available for the area, albeit the rapid development of highways and, to a certain extent, pathways, has left many inaccuracies and conflicts on both maps. The photographs within the walks can also be used as guides to aid passage along the way, as can Items of Interest and scenery descriptions relating to the route.

- EFSTATHIADIS 1:79,000 (with footpaths) ISBN 960 226 5310

- harms IC verlag 1:100,000 Western Crete (includes E4) ISBN 3-927468-16-9

Layout

Each of the three chapters covers a specific topography that is uniquely Cretan. Chapter 1 includes 14 walks, coastal, peninsular, and the immediate hinterland of Crete's dramatic northwest corner. The walks are, by the very nature of the terrain, mainly for the experienced upland enthusiast, although several will no doubt please the coastline rambler, in particular Walk 1, which includes the bedrock Monasterie Gonias. The 20 walks in Chapter 2 traverse not only fertile valleys, picturesque gorges, olive groves, unique woodlands on gentle ridges, rounded foothills that rise to the central, benign massif of Agios (Saint) Dikeos, at 1184m (3885ft) the 'Olympus' of Kissamos and a grandstand beyond compare, but also the southwest coastline of the island, where there is a final walk to the charismatic Monasterie Chrisoskalitissis and the Lagoon of Elafonisos. Chapter 3, with 11 walks, embraces the southern coastline and mountainous heartlands containing and surrounding Kandanos, the capital of Selinos. Whatever your interests when walking, they can be correlated with a specific walk by means of the Special Interests Table that follows this section. Finally, at the end of the book are Appendix 1: A Glossary of Cretan and Greek names, followed by Appendix 2: Further Reading, Appendix 3: Useful Information, and Appendix 4: Summary of Walks.

Chapters 1 to 3

Each chapter begins with a landscape portrait and brief outline of the highlights of each walk. Each walk begins with a fact file, detailing **Distance**, **Height Gain**, **Start/ Finish**, **Grade**, **Walking Time**, **Maps, Accommodation**, **Type of Walk**, and a simple sketch map showing the designated route. The detailed route description includes prominent and permanent features, together with compass bearings if necessary. The directive 'left' or 'right' is invariably confirmed by the instruction, 'i.e. east' or 'i.e. west'. At the end are 'Items of Interest' along the way, each linked to the relevant part of the route description by a number, e.g (1).

The **Grade** is classified from 1 to 4, 1 being a short walk on distinct paths with few or no ascents; 4 is invariably in excess of 10 miles, with steep or long ascents and requiring map and compass skills. **Walking**

Time is calculated by using WW Naismith's established formula: 'For each 3 miles (4.8km) of linear distance allow 1 hour, and should height gain be achieved in that distance add 30 minutes for each 1000ft (305m) of ascent', tempered with my own experiences concerning terrain, weather conditions and convenience stops. This guide was written with pleasure and enjoyment in mind, and as such may err on the slow side. Let each walker proceed with a whistle as they walk, for if you can't whistle you're walking too fast!

CLOTHING AND EQUIPMENT

What do I wear and what equipment should I take for a leisurely ramble along the golden sands of Elafonisos lagoon on a hot summer's day, or for a high-level trek to the summit of Agios Dikeos in a force 8 northwesterly *meltemi*? Three words provide the answer – consider the **conditions** (Overhead, Underfoot, High Level, Low Level) and use your **common sense**.

Conditions Overhead

Kissamos and Selinos, although surrounded on three sides by sea, are not prone to the occasional deluge or thick swirling mist experienced in the 'honey-pot' trekking areas, such as the Lefka Ori (White Mountains) or Psiloritis on the Ida Range. Nor are they subjected to the Siberian cold met on many Munros in Scotland.

Interest	Chapter	Walk
ANTIQUITY	1	2, 3, 5, 6, 7, 9, 13
	2	16, 17, 29
	3	35, 36, 37, 41, 45
DONKEY TRAILS	1	6, 8, 10, 12, 13, 14
	2	15, 16, 17, 21, 22, 23, 25, 27, 28, 29, 31, 34
	3	36, 41, 42, 43, 45
ECCLESIASTICAL (churches, chapels and monasteries)	1	1, 2, 4, 5, 8, 10, 12, 13, 14
	2	15, 16, 17, 23, 25, 26, 27, 28, 29, 30, 31, 33, 34
	3	36, 38, 39, 41, 42, 43, 44, 45
FLORA AND FAUNA	1	1, 2, 3, 4, 6, 8, 9, 10, 12, 13, 14
	2	15, 16, 17, 18, 20, 21, 22, 23, 24, 25, 26, 27, 28, 29, 30, 31, 33, 34
	3	36, 37, 38, 39, 40, 41, 42, 43
GEOLOGY	1	2, 3, 6, 7, 8, 12, 14
	2	15, 16, 18, 22, 23, 27, 32
	3	36, 40, 42, 43
HISTORICAL	1	1, 6, 7, 9, 10, 13, 14
	2	15, 17, 18, 19, 22, 29, 30, 33, 34
	3	35, 36, 38, 41, 44, 45
OLD INDUSTRY	1	6, 7, 12, 13
	2	15, 18, 20, 21, 22, 23, 25, 26, 27, 28, 30, 31, 34
	3	37, 43, 45

PHOTOGRAPHY	1	1, 2, 3, 5, 6, 8, 9, 10, 12, 13, 14,
	2	15, 18, 19, 20, 21, 22, 23, 25,
		26, 27, 28, 29, 30, 31, 34
	3	33, 35, 38, 43, 45
SCENIC BEAUTY	1	1, 2, 3, 5, 6, 8, 9, 10, 11, 12, 14
	2	15, 18, 19, 21, 22, 23, 24, 25,
		26, 27, 29, 30, 31, 32, 34
	3	35, 36, 37, 38, 40, 42, 43, 44, 45
WALKS – CHALLENGING	1	3, 5, 8, 9, 10, 11, 13, 14
	2	15, 17, 19, 21, 23, 25, 27, 28,
		33, 34
	3	36, 37, 38, 42, 43
WALKS – GENTLE	1	2, 6, 7
	2	18, 24, 29
	3	35, 39, 44
WATERCOURSES	1	2, 11, 13, 14
	2	15, 16, 18, 19, 23, 26, 28, 29
	3	35, 38, 43, 45

There are however rare occasions when they, too, experience winter's grip and sometimes summer storms. From November to the end of February the mountains over 610m (2000ft) are liable to have between 8 and 13 days of rain/precipitation, with a snowline around 610m (2000ft) above sea level.

If winter winds, between November and February, threaten, make sure you are suitably clad (see High Level, Winter, later in this section). When considering a trek above 610m, the wind chill factor must always be considered – an increase of 10 miles per hour in wind speed can reduce the temperature from 18°C to 7°C, or in colder conditions from 10°C to –13°C. Bear in mind also the lapse rate – the higher the climb the lower the temperature, for every 1000ft ascended there is a reduction of approximately 3°C.

Temperature and moisture are of prime importance; if both are in agreeable symmetry then the journey will be a pleasure. If not, and the hiker is ill

Imaeri Gramvousa from Agrathos (Walk 9)

prepared and ill equipped, there are twin risks of hypothermia or dehydration/heat exhaustion. Hypothermia can strike if the temperature of the body core drops below 98.4°F in continuous cold and wet conditions. Dehydration or heat exhaustion can be induced by exposing the body, and in particular the head, to excess heat, coupled with an inadequate liquid intake. In Crete both problems can strike the unprepared walker at sea level or on the summit of Vigla 1234m (4049ft)

Conditions Underfoot

While on Rodopou's high eastern and western ridges and the spine of Gramvousa, a high proportion of earth-bound, weather-worn rocks needs to be bypassed as opposed to scrambled over. Such conditions also exist on the ridges and summits of Manna – Profitas Ilias, Leventies, Kastelos – yet the highest in Kissamos, i.e. Agios Dikeos, has a good, wide dirt track from Elos to the chapel-capped summit. The ring of mountains and ridges that overlooks the plateau of Kandanos has similar conditions underfoot to those of Kissamos. In particular the ground-hugging scrub masking angled rocks, between cricket ball and cannon ball size, which can trip you or turn an ankle, should you not 'heed well the placement of the feet'.

Vegetation provides a reliable indicator as to what lies beneath. Avoid patches of bright-green growth, which even in Crete indicates watery conditions, met as Sassalos approaches, Walk 28. Watch out also, particularly when walking on a narrow path through surrounding rock and ankle-high scrub, for snoozing snakes – walking poles are handy in such situations. Choose footwear that will be warm and dry in winter, cool and comfortable in summer. Footwear chosen wisely will lighten the step; take the wrong option and the walk could be a disaster.

31

The abandoned village of Baduriana (Walk 27)

High Level

Winter Walking is not recommended unless you are experienced on high levels in northern Europe. Also, available accommodation is few and far between in winter. Windproof, waterproof and warm anorak/cagoule, waterproof over-trousers or gaiters, woolly hat, gloves/mitts and a survival bag would be needed at altitude. Also high-energy food for a long trek, and emergency rations, such as dried fruit (e.g. apricots), dark chocolate, plus a hot drink. Leave your route details and times with your host.

Summer Wear lightweight clothing and a protective hat, with a windproof/waterproof jacket in the sack, plus a large, water-filled bottle. Those with a fair skin are advised to protect exposed areas with either light clothing or high-factor sun protection.

Low Level

Winter Not recommended, as conditions overhead and underfoot are not conducive to pleasurable, colourful strolls. Beds for the night and tavernas for food are few and far between.

Summer In hot, sunny conditions temperatures average between 24°C and 28°C, rising at times to 40°C in sheltered valleys or on exposed coasts. In such conditions the unprotected walker can suffer from dehydration/heat exhaustion. Essential are a lightweight, broad-brimmed cotton hat, a plentiful supply of drinking water, and a high-factor sun cream for the prevention of sunburn on exposed parts of the walker. The contentious issue of shorts versus lightweight trousers is a matter, I would suggest, of personal preference and individual choice. Do not, as I have occasionally seen in Crete, walk at low levels clad only in swimming trunks and a sack!

Equipment

Veteran and card-carrying pedestrians invariably include a proven talisman in the sack to ward off elemental spirits. It may only be an old woolly sock to keep your water bottle cool, or a phial of *diethyltoluamide* ('diet' for short) to ward off the winged nasties, particularly a type of bad-tempered wasp that raids the many clusters of beehives seen along the way.

SAFETY

Safety is something we must all be aware of, particularly in countries of intense scenic beauty and buildings of intriguing interest such as Crete. A careless or unguarded step could break a bone or tear a tendon, causing a problem for the walker, and if journeying alone, a major problem.

High-level treks and/or rocky coastline explorations are often undertaken in total solitude, so it is essential to possess a basic knowledge of emergency procedures and the equipment needed to minimise discomfort and aid rescue.

Safety Equipment

1) Take a first aid kit, including sterile dressings, zinc tape, antiseptic cream, crepe/elasticated bandages (Tubigrip), scissors/knife and medication. **Medication is for personal use only – do not administer medication to another unless medically qualified.**

2) A basic knowledge of first aid should be carried in the head or in the sack.

3) Pack a knife, torch (with spare bulb and batteries), whistle, spare laces (double up as binding), emergency food and drinking water, survival bag (on mountains), compass, map, paper and pen/pencil.

SAFETY ADVICE

Risks can be reduced by observing a few simple guidelines and using that most underemployed asset – common sense.

1) Prevention is always better than cure. When wildwalking through ground-hugging scrub on an overgrown goat track, always watch where you put your feet.

2) Solitude in the countryside is much sought-after, but with regard to safety should be insured against by informing someone of your route and esti-mated time of return (ETR).

3) Should you be immobilised and require help, use the International Rescue Call:

   six long blasts on a whistle or flashes with a torch, repeated at one-minute intervals; the acknowledging reply – three short blasts at one-minute intervals.

   Should you be without whistle or torch, **SHOUT** using the same code. While waiting for help, utilise the terrain to gain protection from the elements by sheltering on the leeside of outcrops, clumps of vegetation, walls, etc., from wind and rain/snow, or the sun in summer.

4) If with companions, fix your position. This is slightly difficult, as Greek maps do not display grid lines as such, but bearings can be given by using the bearings marked on the perimeter line surrounding the map, e.g. Akrotiri Vouxa (the northern tip of Gramvousa Peninsula) – 23°360′–35°385′. ('Eastings' first, i.e. the immediate vertical perimeter reading to the left of your position, then the number of tenths from the degree figure to your position. Then 'northings' – repeat the procedure using the horizontal degree perimeter markings below the position.) Also put to paper the name and age of the injured person, injury and time sus-tained, general health, clothing including colour, and dispatch an able-bodied companion to the nearest telephone, dwelling or village. Dial **POLICE** to alert and co-ordinate the rescue. When a rescue is requested, the casualty MUST STAY PUT until help arrives.

5) Should you or your companions carry a mobile phone, use it to call for help. Phone number details (correct at the time of writing – I suggest you check before walking) are given in Appendix 3.

CHAPTER 1

Rocky Peninsulas and the
Northwestern Hinterland of Kissamos

Details of the birth of Crete's north-western province of Kissamos, washed on its northern and western coasts by the Cretan Sea, have faded in the mists of memory. In today's Crete, Kissamos, the island's second largest province after the capital Heraklion, stands proud. Through many millennia varied races and cultures have cast their eyes over and waved their weapons at this fertile, prosperous northwestern portal of Crete. Achaeans (from a state of Ancient Greece), Romans, Byzantines, Venetians and Turks have through the centuries dominated Kissamos. All were oppressive, but many turned their commercial and administrative strengths to benefit the area, seen in the growth of towns and cities. When the Romans dominated (67BC–95AD) internal power struggles ceased and economic growth blossomed.

Important city-states were Phalasarna, Polyrinia, Kastelli, Agneion, Inahorion and Diktynnaion. Polyrinia, with its two ports of Phalasarna and Kastelli, was the most influential, because it did not resist the Roman incursion instigated by Emperor Hadrian. A statue of the Roman General Metellus was erected, and Polyrinia was rewarded accordingly. Walks 6, 7, 13, 17 and 26 (the latter two in Chapter 2) visit four of these cities, where excavations can be seen, while the Museum of Antiquities in Kastelli displays many artefacts from these ancient settlements.

Rodopou Rock above the Gulf of Kastelli (Walk 5)

In tandem with the visible historical evidence throughout Kissamos there are varied scenic walks, pleasing and unique to Crete, that challenge, reward and delight, be they mountain ascents or coastline strolls.

THE AREA

Rodopou Peninsula

Linked to mainland Kissamos, at Kolimbari in the east and Nopigia in the west, this forbidding mass of rock provides the eastern bracket for the Gulf of Kissamos. On average it is 5.5km (3½ miles) wide, and at Mouri, its highest point, it rises to 751m (2464ft) and spears north for 20.25km (15¾ miles) to Akrotiri (Cape) Spatha. Five kilometres (3¼ miles) southeast of Spatha is Roman Diktynnaion, built in the fifth century BC and dedicated to Diktynna–Artemis. Today little remains save a temple that was fronted with columns, plus an altar surrounded by the remains of several temples from the seventh and sixth centuries BC. Further west a large statue of the Roman Emperor Trajan and an image of the goddess Venus were discovered and now rest in Gonias Monastery.

Habitation consists of villages, all within the southern third of the peninsula, all essentially agricultural, with olives, vines and glasshouse production, plus an abundance of goats. The main village is Rodopou, gateway to the deserted northern quadrant. The most attractive village, with food and accommodation, and the hub for most of the following walks, is flower-strewn, friendly Afrata, overlooking the Gulf of Chania, 2km (1¼ miles) east from Rodopou.

Gramvousa Peninsula

Originating from Doris in mainland Greece, the Dorians (1100–480BC) brought to Crete a dialect of elongated vowels (not unlike Scots), skilled metalworkers, and an overpowering inclination to subjugate the indigenous population and build settlements exposed to the sea. They apparently built a Dorian sanctuary astride the rocky point of Gramvousa.

After the Dorian influence waned, Crete experienced the might of Rome, then the uncompromising hand of Islam, and was later to suffer further when the Republic of Venice bought Crete for 'a widow's mite'. Venetians were present from the 1200s to 1669, creating fine towns where science and the arts flourished, but sadly at the expense, physically and financially, of the population, who, being Cretans, revolted. In 1584 an imposing castle rose on the adjacent islet of Imeri Gramvousa, built, ironically, by enslaved Cretans for the Venetians. The castle's remains can be seen today, as can adjacent St George's Church.

As late as the 1980s Crete's northwestern extremity remained an undiscovered wilderness. Few, save goatherds, archaeologists, or those who came by sea, explored or enjoyed its mountainous spine, shimmering blue shallows, the pristine sands of Tigani Bay, once a haunt of pirates, or the circlet of island gems gracing the rocky apex of Akrotiri (Cape) Vouxa. There were few routes of passage, save an occasional animal track along and above the more benign east coast. Today, for better or worse, a dirt road of 11km (7 miles) overlooking the sea and Rodopou Peninsula, has been blasted north from the colourful and expanding village of Kaliviani to the col above Balos Bay. Much to the delight of motorised travellers – providing the vehicle is hired – and the wayfarer – providing they avoid the dust clouds – there is much to see and discover from this panoramic way.

THE WALKS

Fourteen diverse walks, encompassing the two intriguing, scenically unique peninsulas of Rodopou and Gramvousa bracketing the Gulf of Kissamos, are included in Chapter 1, varying from a 5km (3¼ mile) introductory stroll from Kolimbari to Afrata, to a serious there-and-back trek of 32km (20¼ miles), which includes sections of wildwalking and exposure over the entire length of Gramvousa Peninsula. **Walk 1** provides sea views over the Gulf of Chania and inland sightings of the Lefka Ori (White Mountains) as we pass by the holy Monastery of Gonias, and above it the Cadets' Monument, ascending to the colourful villages of Upper and Lower Afrata. **Walk 2** is strong on views, flora, fauna, geology,

geography, two churches – one clinging to a cliff – a gorge and a bay to swim in. **Walk 3**, with nautical connections, is a serious affair, searching for Ellinospilios, the 'Hall of Tombs', while **Walk 4** legs it over Rodopou's ravine-strewn central spine to its western shoreline at Ravdouha. **Walk 5** confirms that 'Rodopou is spectacular', as are the landscapes inland and overlooking the Gulf of Kissamos. **Walks 6 and 7** search Kastelli and its surrounds for those who trod this way centuries past. **Walk 8** treks to Tigani, the legendary 'Bay of Pirates' lagoon, and **Walk 9** goes 10km (6 miles) further to the wild beauty of Crete's ethereal extremity at Vouxa – a summer walk with the option to return by boat! **Walk 10** ascends Gramvousa's pinnacle by church and chapel, and **Walk 11** takes the experienced mountaineer in search of solitude. **Walk 12** is an inland journey through olives and vines to Monasterie Tilifos below Geroskinos. **Walk 13A** provides a contrasting, coastal and mountain journey of archaeological interest to Phalasarna's 'high and dry' harbour; an alternative, **13B**, equally scenic, extends from Falasarna to Kaliviani. To conclude with a bang, **Walk 14** includes a direct ascent to Manna's chapel-capped summit, grandstand of Profitas Ilias, for an eagle's-eye view of all that is Chapter 1.

WALK 1

Through Mud and Blood to
Green Hills Beyond

Kolimbari, Gonias Monasterie,
Cadets' Monument, Afrata

Distance	5km (3¼ miles)
Height Gain	300m (984ft)
Start/Finish	Kolimbari, at the SE corner of Rodopou Peninsula/Afrata
Grade	2
Walking Time	1½ hours
Maps	EFSTATHIADIS 1:79,000 CHANIA (with footpaths)
	ISBN 960 226 5310
	harms IC verlag 1:100,000 Western Crete (includes E4)
	ISBN 3–927468–16–9
Accommodation	Hotels and rooms at Kolimbari and Afrata

By rocky coastline, roads, stony tracks and pathways, ascend to picturesque Afrata above the gorge guiding the River Troulos into the Gulf of Chania.

The Route

Leave the bustling centre of Kolimbari from the highway crossroads, walking N and NW on the footpath to the picturesque harbour, now expanding with extra basins for fishing boats and leisure craft. Old and new are worth a prowl before rejoining the olive-tree-lined road N to the charismatic Monastery Odogitrias Kirias Gonias (1) and its adjacent Orthodox Academy (1A) – an arched building with hints of Catalunyan architecture. Behind stands a new building and a large cross, soon passed, as the curving road ascends left above cliffs and the blue waters of the Gulf of Chania.

Continue N with the rising road to a signed junction 'North – Afrata, West – Soldiers' (Cadets') Monument' (2). Take the W way, a looping road of 1km (²⁄₃ mile) from which the white and olive-green oasis of Afrata can be seen, some 2km (1¼ miles) NNW through a V in the hills, leading up to the simple marble and brass monument dedicated to 10 cadets who gave their lives defending their country. Views S and E encompass Chania Bay, Isle Saint Theodori, Akrotiri Peninsula, and beyond Kolimbari and Maleme (3), the coastal battlefield of 1941, backed by the white mountains of the Lefka Ori.

Contrary to 'paths' marked on the Greek maps, **there are no footpaths on the ground that lead to Afrata from the memorial site.** The paths that do appear lead,

Kolimbari harbour

The Cadets'
Monument

unfortunately, to rubbish tips and 2m high wire fences. To avoid frustration return to the coastal road which zigzags for 2½km (1½ miles) ascending 200m to Afrata. **(A dust and stone track does ascend through the gorge leading north to Afrata, beyond the quarry. Unfortunately passage is impractical, due to a high wiremesh fence with no gates. No matter how inviting the gorge appears, do not be tempted.)**

Continue N and SW via the wriggling, ascending roadside verge, through olive groves and vineyards – a walk that provides superb views before reaching the pristine white walls of floral Afrata nestling beneath the central ridge of Rodopou Peninsula and the stark rock face of Troulos 430m (1411ft).

Beyond Apano (Upper) Afrata stands the equally attractive Kato (Lower) Afrata, above the narrow, descending rocky Troulos/Afrata Gorge and a small bay by blue waters – Walk 2.

Items of Interest
(1) **GONIAS MONASTERY**, 13th and 17th century, arose from a simple cloister linked to the temple of

Dictyna Artemis–Vritomartis, the ancient goddess of Western Crete. It is said that the monastery was founded when in 1618 the Virgin Mary came to the holy monk Vlasios to ask him to raise a church on a place of her choosing. In 1634 the church was completed and flourished, but disaster struck on the 13 June 1645, when invading Turks pillaged and fired the cloister. The dual purpose of this extraordinary Cretan monastery was determined that June day, for not only is it a church that exhibits internal beauty and religious charisma, it also became the focal point of and inspiration for Crete's resistance to foreign intrusion throughout subsequent centuries.

Open to visitors 8am–12.30pm, and in summer also 4pm–8pm; closed Saturday. Men must wear long trousers, women long skirts or trousers. No internal photographs.

(1A) **ORTHODOX ACADEMY**, founded 1965 by the Metropolitan Bishop of Kissamos district. Its purpose is to encourage understanding of the economic, cultural and social situation of Crete.

(2) **CADETS' MONUMENT**. Dedicated to the 'fallen cadets', a synopsis reads, 'It was on this rise on 20 May 1941 that 300 first-year Military Cadets defended their homeland and in this way played their part in the legendary Battle of Crete.' Ten cadets fell during the battle, although eleven names are inscribed on the marble cube of the monument.

(3) **BATTLE OF MALEME.** May 1941 saw the parachuting German invaders descend on the coastal plain surrounding the nearby township of Maleme, which fell with many casualties on either side after bitter fighting. Further parachute attacks laid waste to Nohia, Drapanias and Kastelli, again with many deaths in and after the battles. Maleme is today the site of the German cemetery.

WALK 2

A Stroll of Two Halves –
Above and Below Afrata

Apano Afrata, Saint Konstantinos,
Afrata Gorge, Gulf of Chania

Distance	6km (3¾ miles)
Height Gain	180m (591ft)
Start/Finish	Afrata /Afrata
Grade	1
Walking Time	2 hours
Maps	EFSTATHIADIS 1:79,000 CHANIA (with footpaths) ISBN 960 226 5310
	harms IC verlag 1:100,000 Western Crete (includes E4) ISBN 3–927468–16–9
Accommodation	Afrata – Hotel Minore and rooms

Although short in length, this 'bantam' stroll, from the eastern-ridge side of Rodopou Peninsula to the Gulf of Chania shoreline and back, is full of views and habitats, flora and fauna, geology and geography. A small church stands on the high plateau below the sugarloaf summit of Troulos, another clings to the sheer wall of the Afrata Gorge. We stroll from village to plateau, then descend through the narrow Afrata Gorge (*farangi*) to the luxury of a grassy bank by a sand and shingle beach and bay, a *cantina*, loungers and toilet. This beach can get busy on summer weekends. It is either one walk or two strolls.

The Route
From Apano Afrata descend NE with the narrow, winding tarmac lane, passing the Hotel Minore, to the colourful lower village of Kato Afrata. Continue, beyond the flower-bedecked village square and Taverna Roxanne, to

the acute, descending-right elbow beyond. Here a fingerpost 'Ayios Konstantinos' directs left, i.e. NW, on a dirt track for approximately 1km (²/₃ mile) to the tiny white church of Saint Konstantinos, overlooked by Rodopou's central ridge and rocky Troulos' 430m (1411ft). Surrounded by trees, W of the road, the church provides fine views S and SE over the Gulf of Chania to the snow-capped mountains of the Lefka Ori. After admiring church and views return to the village fingerpost – 'Ayios Konstantinos'.

Walk 2

St Konstantinos
TROULOS▲
430m
Afrata
N
Rodopos
0   1   2
km

Descend overall E via a series of zigzags to reach a T-junction, turn right to walk E on the quiet asphalt road, passing the last, very attractive house before descending seawards for 1km (²/₃ mile) through the small but spectacular gorge (1). Never claustrophobic, unlike some of the larger Sfakia gorges, this somewhat diminutive *farangi* plunges into the Gulf (Kolpos) of Chania. A tiny bay, pebbles, stones and sand, plus the proud flag of Greece and warm seawater, greet the walker. It's a fine spot in which to relax, surrounded by sea, gorge and high ridge.

Return to Afrata, ascending through the gorge, whose incline encourages frequent stops to study the flaking, pitted structure of the rock, the antics of the resident raptors, from hawks to the large, white-splashed eagles (2) that soar above and nest on the rocky walls, and the farmed pigs, sheep and goats below the northern wall. At the upper mouth of the gorge a series of steps leads to a small white chapel clinging to the north wall beneath a rather precarious overhang. As with the majority of Greek churches, the door is always unlocked.

The return to the village is via the winding outward road, and for those requiring refreshment Roxanne's Taverna is conveniently placed.

Afrata Gorge into the Gulf of Chania

Items of Interest

(1) **AFRATA/TROULOS GORGE**. To avoid confusion with Afrata's fenced southern gorge, I have added 'Troulos' to the name, as the water course from rocky Troulos runs through the gorge into the Gulf of Chania. When the present road to Afrata was under construction, human and mammals' bones were found, confirming that Crete was inhabited in Mesolithic times (Middle Stone Age), although this theory apparently prompts some disagreement, as other historians believe that Crete's first inhabitants were Neolithic, i.e. 6000–2500BC. The gorge walls are composed of soft rock, lime, chalk and sandstone – not to be climbed or scrambled, but home to alkaline-loving plants and birds of prey.

(2) **RESIDENT RAPTORS**. In addition to the 26 local species, from falcons and buzzards to eagles, that are seen above and nesting in the narrow confines of the Afrata Gorge, there are also 19 species of migrants that visit Rodopou's varied coastline and hinterland.

WALK 3

To the 'Hall of Tombs'

Afrata, Ellinospilios, Afrata

Distance	6km (3¾ miles)
Height Gain	50m (164ft)
Start/Finish	Afrata/Afrata
Grade	3 (4 over the shoreline rocks for several hundred metres to and from the cave entrance)
Walking Time	3–4 hours
Maps	EFSTATHIADIS 1:79,000 CHANIA (with footpaths) ISBN 960 226 531 0
	harms IC verlag 1:100,000 Western Crete (includes E4) ISBN 3–927468–16–9
Accommodation	Afrata – Hotel Minore and rooms

From the Afrata villages this there-and-back walk leads, via tarmac and dirt lanes, to a stepped, prepared path leading to and from rocky, cave-pitted sea stacs, cliffs and bays with razor-sharp stones that make up this eastern shoreline of Rodopou. The passage from the prepared path to shore requires rock-scrambling experience, care and caution. This walk can be split into sections depending on ability. For those who can handle the complete journey it is a unique and highly rewarding half-day. **For experienced cavers it is a must, but do not enter the Ellinospilios cave unless you are experienced, properly equipped (that includes several hundred metres of stout string, a powerful torch and spare batteries and plenty of drinking water) and accompanied by experienced companions.**

The Route

Walk N with the narrow tarmac road through Upper Afrata, descending past an exposed face of calcareous

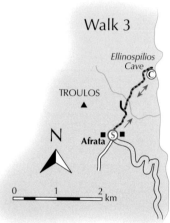

rock (*potamida*) to Lower Afrata's village square and the Roxanne Taverna. Ahead, to the east, is the deep, riven cleft of the narrow Afrata/Troulos Gorge beyond the twisting asphalt road. Pass all the roadside houses bar two to reach a T-junction. Afrata Gorge and 'Seaside' are to the right, our route is left onto a concrete road rising W and N through the olive-clad valley between a shore-line ridge and the central spine of Rodopou Peninsula.

With scrub left and olives right, take a right-hand ascending dirt track, then a north-bound twintrack rising SE for several hundred metres before swinging left past a large new building on the right as we rise NE and ENE. Immediately beyond, turn right, i.e. E, to pass through a wiremesh gate onto a prepared path, overgrown in places, with mesh-fencing left, rustic wooden fence right, for approximately 100m to a sturdy wooden gate. Beyond, a stepped and stone-bordered footpath with wooden seats crosses the sloping hillside overlooking the Gulf of Chania. Descend, passing well-placed seats, beneath shady clumps of *koomera* (a native shrub), with leisurely viewing of this Cretan canvas.

Continue with the paint-dotted path that provides bird's-eye views of the shoreline. All too soon it ends, beyond a pathside rock with a palm-sized red paint blotch. Here a lengthy wiremesh fence can be seen running seawards towards a trio of jutting cliffs/stacs.

I have been to these cliffs and stacs via the fence – passage is rough and unstable, so do not pass through the fence unless you have experience and ability.

Admire, then return on the outward stepped pathway and dirt tracks to the T-junction below Kato Afrata.

For the capable and experienced, continue towards the trio of jutting stacs to meet the wire fence ahead, pass through and turn right. The fence, such as it is, is now on the right. Descend E on a narrow, scrub-lined path with care, as overgrown support wires from the fence can trip the walker. The fenceside journey to the first rock stac is steep and stony, and a right-angle turn requires hands-on assistance for a brief scramble before the first large outcrop above a copse of shelter trees by the fence. From here leave the fence half-left to round the stac's landward side, contouring N above the restless shoreline on the right. Underfoot on low scrub and naked rock, crisscrossed by goat tracks, walk towards the mouth of what appears to be a sizeable cave in the cliff face of a rocky promontory at the northern end of the bay, 50m or so below.

From the first stac to this possible 'Ellinospilios' is a short 250m, but it is not however our target. It is only a few metres deep and obviously, by the floor covering, a favoured goat shelter. Note, some 10m from the shallow entrance, a stone-built semicircular wall. The significance of this cave and stone wall is that they provide sightings S, over the curved wall, into the rocky bay below, 20–25m above sea level, to a small cave entrance on the southern arc and one in the centre.

The following should only be attempted by experienced scramblers, as rocks are rounded and slippery, or jagged and razor sharp.

Access to the bay floor and the two cave entrances is achieved by contouring, via goat tracks S, to pass below the eastern face of a freestanding rock stac. Once past veer left, i.e. E, to descend to a 2m-high boulder, balanced on rocks the size of footballs. From this boulder descend further E, then half-left to the shoreline and after 15m stop and look left. The mouth of the cave on the southern arc of the bay should now be visible 20m ahead and left. Information from Afrata residents 'ELLINOSPILIOS is at hand' was confirmed, its entrance smaller than anticipated (1). Five metres into the cave the

*Cave entrance of
Ellinospilios*

passage narrows from floor to rock ceiling. The smooth white and pale-brown calcareous rock demands a crawl or belly-wriggle of several metres to gain access to the enlarging and extensive chamber beyond. **Note the warning in the introduction to this walk.**

The third cave – at the centre of the rocky bay – is shallow and of little interest. Return to the freestanding 2m boulder and climb W below the first-met rock stac above the bay on its S side to reach the small copse of fenceside shelter trees. Follow with care the fence that guided our outward journey to join the stepped way over the sloping hillside. Admire the sea views and the mountain canvas of the Lefka Ori.

Pass through the gates onto the pathway, passing the large building of the outward journey to turn left onto the tracks, lanes and tarmac leading SW to the T-junction below Kato Afrata.

Items of Interest

(1) **ELLINOSPILIOS CAVE**. A small and narrow entrance hides a cave of great stature, hewn out of chalk and limestone, said to be 25m in height with a floor that strides 160m into the hillside. A central rock column leads to a side area referred to as the 'Hall of Tombs'. It was at this place that further excavations yielded both human and animal remains. Stalactites and stalagmites abound (see also Cave of Saint Sophia, Walk 18).

WALK 4

Afrata to Ravdouha

Afrata, Astratigos, Aspra Nera, Ravdouha

Distance	7½km (4¾ miles)
Height Loss	300m (984ft)
Start/Finish	Afrata/Ravdouha
Grade	2
Walking Time	2½ hours
Maps	EFSTATHIADIS 1:79,000 CHANIA (with footpaths)
	ISBN 960 226 531 0
	harms IC verlag 1:100,000 Western Crete (includes E4)
	ISBN 3–927468–16–9
Accommodation	Afrata, Apano Ravdouha and Kato Ravdouha

This quiet ramble utilises country roads and lanes over Rodopou Peninsula's central ridge. Clothed by ubiquitous olive and scrub, it provides grandstand vistas of Crete's northwest coastline and hinterland. Sharing the country road with vehicles is not the nightmare experienced at home, and underfoot it's a bonus.

The Route

Walk SSW from Afrata, past two flower-bedecked tavernas on the right, via the ascending, broom-lined Astratigos road SW and S for 2km (1¼ miles), surrounded by ridges, rock valleys and olive groves. Over the shoulder of the central ridge, expanding Astratigos reveals colourful buildings, typified by the central church. Continue S, by fields, shady trees and overhanging rocks, to a junction where the tarmac road sweeps right to Rodopou. Transfer to the stony dirt track, S and SW, towards tiny Aspra Nera, on an undulating track through extensive olive groves (1) to the scattered village of red pantiles.

At the asphalt road swing right, i.e. W, descending to a major crossroads – 'Rodopou' right, 'Chania' left, 'Ravdouha' 3km (nearly 2 miles) straight ahead – along with a directional waymark 'Wave on the Rock – Ravdouha Beach'. The 3km hike is via a scenically pleasing, undulating tarmac road (not shown on the EFSTATHIADIS map) that hurries W–NW–SW. After a widening waymarked junction with the Kamara road, ascend W through olive groves to the two thriving halves of Apano Ravdouha, overlooking the Gulf of Kissamos and the tiny harbour at Kato Ravdouha 200m (656ft) below.

Should you wish to descend to the shoreline, well worth a visit, walk S to the willow tree by the impressive Holy Trinity Church on the left. Turn right by its cemetery onto the rapidly descending zigzag, passing, halfway down, the start of Walk 5 just above the charming Chapel of Saint Marina (2). As the shoreline approaches, a fork in the road directs S and N, indicating the services available; the stroll in either direction is

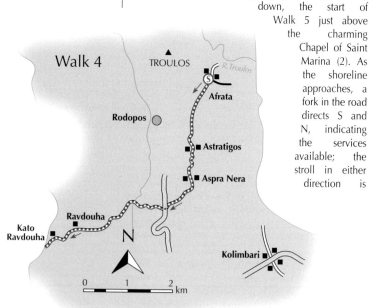

Saint Marina – look for murals

most rewarding. Admire the olive groves, the gardens by the seashore (3), overlooked by colourful, fissured cliffs and strange formations of calcareous rock probing into the sea, then gaze W to the serrated skyline of the Gramvousa Peninsula.

Items of Interest

(1) Growing alongside the tracks is rue (*Ruta chalepensis*), favoured by Hippocratian doctors as an antitoxin to combat snake bites and hysteria. Other uses, when sweetened, would rid the patient of tapeworms and internal parasites. Sage is also seen, a herb favoured by the medical fathers Pliny, Hippocrates and others as a diuretic and disinfectant.

(2) **SAINT MARINA** is a chapel in the rock, clamped above a communal wash house, its walls and arched ceiling illuminated with expertly restored classic murals that equal the masterpieces gracing Saint Gorgios at Anidri (Walk 38) and Saint Mamas by Kandanos (Walk 41).

(3) **HERBS and PLANTS**. A favoured place in spring for wild artichoke (*Cynara cardunculus*), sought-after in local tavernas. Also thriving is the carob tree (*Ceratonia siliqua*), which produces the carob bean from which *charouba*, a local soft drink was made, traditionally chilled with snow from the Lefka Ori mountains.

WALK 5

Rodopou is Spectacular

Kato Ravdouha, Saint Marina, Nopigia

Distance	7km (4½ miles)
Height Gain	150m (492ft), if starting from sea level 250m (820ft)
Start/Finish	The elbow in the zigzag road between Ravdouha and Kato Ravdouha, immediately above Saint Marina chapel/Nopigia
Grade	3–4 depending on weather
Walking Time	3–4 hours to absorb the surroundings
Maps	EFSTATHIADIS 1:79,000 CHANIA (with footpaths) ISBN 960 226 531 0
	harms IC verlag 1:100,000 Western Crete ISBN 3-927468-16-9
Accommodation	Ravdouha and Nopigia (and camping)

For enthusiastic hillwalkers, a spectacular, far-seeing linear trek along the western flanks of the prominent Rodopou Peninsula. Initially by a zigzag road, then traversing steep, exposed slopes above the shoreline over rock and scrub, marked in places with small cairns and/or painted stones and rock, gradually descending with flower-lined paths, crossing small, tree-filled gullies and oleander beds to the shoreline leading to the amphitheatre heralding Nopigia. Matching our colourful route are magnificent views west over the blue waters of Kolipos Kissamou (Kastelli Bay) to the awesome peninsula of Gramvousa, and south over the fertile coastal plain to the mountains and gorges of Kissamos.

The Route

Start from the sharp-angled bend above Saint Marina (1), as a southern route allows the walker to enjoy 180° of diverse land and seascapes. A thin dirt and stone path

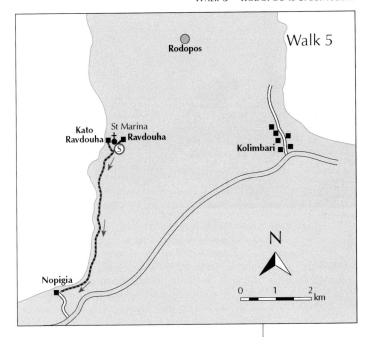

passes, almost immediately, through a tiny olive grove with a wire fence on the right and red waymarked rock on the left. **Passage S on the narrow but clearly visible path requires care as loose stones underfoot can be troublesome. The steep slopes dropping dramatically 100/150m (328/492ft) to the rocky shoreline, overlooked by the great wedge of Jurassic rock jutting into Kastelli Bay and Gramvousa Peninsula, demand attention.**

Frequent paint waymarks, interspersed with small stone cairns, assist passage around, under and over sizeable rocky outcrops, some capped with hillside trees, leading to a high wiremesh fence at right angles to our path. Pass through an easily opened gate, clearly marked with an empty plastic bottle, onto a wider pathway under an overhang above the westerly Jurassic wedge. Although exposed, this stretch provides seats on the rocks

53

Rodopou over Kastelli Gulf to central Kissamos

from which to admire the views west of the bay and rocky profiles of Gramvousa.

Continue S from the exposed rocks, descending slightly, before an overall descent to the shoreline ahead. Now we are crossing the first of three picturesque shoulders of Rodopou's central N–S ridge. Visible ahead is at least half of Kissamou's uniquely varied landscape (2). Underfoot, all three sloping shoulders to the sea are carpeted (in spring and early summer) with coloured gorse and a scatter of tiny, blue-scented lavender. Waymarks abound as the path ascends and descends to the shoreline; Nopigia, our goal, is clearly in sight.

Approximately 100m (328ft) above the sea the pathway nips in and out of sea-bound dry gullies, the third and last quite narrow and steep in places. Filled with scrubby dwarf conifers and gorse, occupied invariably by sheltering goats, it requires perhaps the use of the fifth appendage. Then spill onto a small beach to gaze around this perfect Cretan panorama. A deep, tree-clad gully leads to a pebble beach with a derelict church to the left. Passing through rock and soft stone, by small cairns and waymarks, reach and penetrate a dense plantation covering a half *strema* (1000 sq m) of oleander.

Once through, two waymarked paths, close to the stone- and bamboo-scattered beach, are on offer through a clearing. The one onto the beach I would not recommend. Beyond an old building leave the shoreline by a path over pebble and driftwood, passing and ascending between two prominent water-sculptured outcrops onto a distinct tree-lined path that wends its way S around inlets.

Although the scrub-lined paths are narrow they remain distinct for the next 500m before emerging onto an 'olive-waste' strewn field above a clearing and wide dirt/stone vehicle track. ▶

Continue descending to the shore. Note an angled shelf of partially submerged geometrical rocks, before passing a pristine white chapel left. With the waters of Kolpos Kissamou lapping the strange-shaped rocks on the right, and giant, yellow-spotted bees seeking pollen from the gargantuan, blue-flowered thistles on the left, asphalt underfoot and a bank of oleander ahead, we pass 'Polo rock', Guernsey and Friesian cows, to reach Nopigia's amphitheatre (3) and shady campsite, heralding journeys end.

At the time of research rumours were rife that metal stakes marking this point indicated a proposed site for a large hotel complex. If planning permission is granted an alternative route to bypass the complex would be provided.

Items of Interest
(1) **SAINT MARINA**. The chapel in the rock – See Walk 4.

(2) **LANDSCAPE**. From the white coastal villages and the township of Kastelli south to the gorges and mountains, west from Rokka and Malathiros to Leventies, Topolia and the dome of Profitas Ilias beyond the fertile Tiflos valley.

(3) **NOPIGIA**. A Minoan settlement of indigenous inhabitants and immigrants from Asia Minor grew and prospered west of present-day Nopigia and the River Koleni. The amphitheatre seen today is bolted and barred, prompting me to inquire from two knowledgeable Cretan friends its age, as I had witnessed one spring morning an Ancient Greek dancing class slowly and rhythmically 'taking to the floor'. One friend placed its age around 25 years, the other about 10 years, not centuries!, old.

WALKS 6 AND 7

Kastelli – Ancient and Modern

Trahilos Fishing Harbour, Mavros Molos, Kastelli's Roman, Trojan, Venetian and Turkish Antiquities

Distance	5.25km (3¼ miles)
Height Gain	50m (164ft)
Start/Finish	Kastelli's fishing harbour (Trahilos)/Kastelli
Grade	1
Walking Time	2 hours, depending on time spent wandering around Kastelli
Maps	EFSTATHIADIS 1:79,000 CHANIA (with footpaths) ISBN 960 226 531 0
	harms IC verlag 1:100,000 Western Crete ISBN 3–927468–16–9
Accommodation	Kastelli – a wide range

Kissamos (the ancient name), or Kastelli (the modern name), is the port and gateway of Western Crete – a friendly, cosmopolitan city that exhibits its at times violent history with dignity.

Walk 6 journeys from the small fishing harbour of Trahilos, via an interesting shoreline walk south to the ancient Minoan port of Mavros Molos, guarded by a breakwater of huge black rocks (*mavro* means black), before a browse through the streets and alleys of Kastelli in search of visible evidence of Roman, Venetian, Turkish, and more recent invaders.

Walk 7 can be either from the fishing harbour to Mavros Molos, or from Mavros Molos into Kastelli in search of Greco-Roman, Venetian and Turkish occupation, and a visit to the archaeological museum.

The Route
From the picturesque fishing and pleasure-boat harbour (refreshments available), just off the main road S of the

ferryboat harbour, walk S past the bobbing craft on a path/thin track alongside the Gulf of Kastelli. We are not only in search of fine scenic views, but also items of interest en route, for many and varied invaders have arrived on these shores through the centuries.

Follow the thin trod, picking your route along the scrub-laden foreshore, with a little bamboo on the right, past several rocky inlets. The walking is not difficult, often over flat, slabby rock, as we progress SSE towards the mysteries of Mavros Molos and its black, retaining harbour wall. Initially we meet an old 'modern' harbour (1) whose disused and broken quayside of stone and cement has not withstood the stormy waters as well as Mavros Molos. Before and beyond this point it would be of interest to examine the slabs of ancient stone (2) underfoot.

Above this redundant harbour rise right onto a road to join the main Kastelli road for a short stretch alongside a walled garden of rest, with seats and water (its gates were all locked when we passed by). Once past, turn sharp left for a few metres, walking between the gardens and a newish beachside hotel, to the fine sandy bay alongside the sickle of jagged black boulders (3) probing north into the invariably calm waters of the Gulf of Kissamos – a gulf framed by the dramatic peninsulas of Gramvousa to the west and Rodopou to the east.

Walks 6 and 7

Trahilos
fishing harbour
Walk 6

N

Mavros Molos
(Minoan Port)

Walk 7

Kastelli

Venetian Castle
Turkish
Water Fountain
Museum

0   1   2 km

Mavros Molos prehistoric harbour

Walk beside the tamarisk trees of the western bay to reach a road coming towards the shore on the right. Cross an overgrown waterway via an arched wooden bridge leading to a constant fringe of tavernas, *cafenion*, etc., alongside the shoreline. Approach Taverna Papadki, beneath two widespread tamarisk trees, beyond which a small jetty points seawards, crowned by a marble memorial dated 20 May 1944 bearing the names of 15 Cretan partisans. At the jetty's north end a jumble of broken rocks and concrete rises above the waters of the bay – the remains of a harbour demolished by retreating German forces in 1944.

The shoreline walkway is supposedly 'vehicle prohibited'. It does however allow fine views N of the Gulf of Kastelli framed by the peninsulas of Gramvousa left and Rodopou right. Continue E to meet the last taverna, Cellar Fish Restaurant (at the time of writing). Before this, turn right towards the town centre, leaving the waterside, then first right to meet the turreted walls and remains of the Venetian Castle (4). Closer to the central square a 2 metre wide base rises for 3 metres to the higher turreted section.

Follow the wide road into the central square, with bus station, bars, tavernas, hotels and shops, teenagers and motorbikes – invariably a place of bustle, centrally graced by the recently renovated archaeological museum, impressive on the outside, more so inside. In 2004 its entire contents were in storage (including the Greco-Roman mosaic floor excavated from behind the Health Centre Hospital).

Leave the square E, i.e. left, at the corner of Castell Hotel to walk E along the rather narrow, shaded street of 'KAMOYUH'. 135 paces from the square, turn left into a small, cool, stepped, tree-and-house-shaded enclave containing a fascinating, classical, stone Turkish water fountain (5) in the shadow of an old Turkish house, surrounded by two flower beds. From this quiet, cool place return to the Museum Square for rest and refreshment.

Walk S from the Museum Square, cross the main thoroughfare (with care) and walk 50 paces or so to the Health Centre Hospital. On the S and W sides of the hospital can be seen recent excavations that have exposed mosaics and the foundations of many buildings dating from the Greco-Roman Period (6).

Fossil shells by Mavros Molos

59

Turkish water fountain

Leave the archaeological site to walk W for one block, then swing right, i.e. N, to meet the main central road through Kastelli. Cross this busy road and immediately ahead a second excavation site can be seen, with a third site one block W and one block N by a street named 'ΒΑΤΛΑΝΤΑΝΗ'.

This site may be a good place to end your exploration of Kastelli, although there are other glimpses into the past, such as the Archbishop's House – the choice is yours. It's an easy return N along the shoreline on our outward pathway to the fishing harbour – our starting point.

Items of Interest

(1) This harbour and quayside has been replaced by the present larger and deeper ferryboat terminal north of our starting point at Trahilos, handling the majority of marine traffic to and from rapidly expanding Kastelli.

(2) A scatter of sizeable fossilised mollusc shells can be seen underfoot, in various states of perfection, embedded in the rock.

(3) **MAVROS MOLOS**. Legend has it that Agamemnon, returning from the Trojan Wars in the 12th century BC, cast anchor here while he journeyed to Polyrinia (Walk 17) to give thanks to the goddess Artemis for his Trojan victories.

(4) **VENETIAN CASTLE**. For 465 years Crete was under the yoke of the Venetians, who in the 13th century commissioned the pirate 'Rescatore' to build a castle (Casteli di Kissamo). In 1570 it was assailed by rebelling Cretans; in 1595 it was severely shaken by an earthquake and was rebuilt by the Venetian Contarini. In 1646 the castle and Crete fell to the heavy hand of the Turks, who later governed with a rod of iron until 1823, when Commissioner Tobazis and 600 soldiers forced them to surrender. The castle changed hands many times until 1897, when finally the Turks returned to Turkey.

(5) **TURKISH WATER FOUNTAIN**. Four-sided, multi-angled roof topped by a circular stone cone and dated 1520 – it provides a constant flow of cold, clear water.

(6) **GRECO-ROMAN PERIOD**. As with Polyrinia, Kastelli, a trading city, also saw and appreciated the advantages of a trading 'alliance' with the occupying Romans (69BC–395). The city grew and prospered, as never before or since, throughout Byzantine times (395–1204). The finest examples of the Greco-Roman period, statues of emperors Hadrian and Satyr, can be seen in the Museum of Kissamos.

WALK 8

To the Bay of Pirates

*Kaliviani, Balos Beach Hotel,
Balos Col, Bay of Tigani*

Distance	22km (13½ miles) there and back
Height Gain	250m (820ft)
Start/Finish	Kaliviani – Saint Nicholoas church
Grade	4 there and back, 3 travelling one way by ferry
Walking Time	7 hours
Maps	EFSTATHIADIS 1:79,000 CHANIA (some footpaths), ISBN 960 226 531 0
	harms IC verlag 1:100,000 Western Crete (includes E4) ISBN 3–927468–16–9
Accommodation	Kastelli and Kaliviani – hotels, apartments, rooms

A long walk. Underfoot, dirt road and stone pathway, ascending and descending steps to Balos Bay, sandy beach, the lagoon and Tigani. Here are gourmet helpings of Cretan sights and sounds, as the dirt road north reveals flora and fauna, seashore, and the flanks of Geroskinos – Gramvousa's highest mountain. If Tigani lagoon is your destination, as opposed to viewing it from the col above, be prepared for a zigzag stepped descent to the fine sands and turquoise waters.

The Route

Leave flower-laden Kaliviani at the northern end of its main 'street', between the *ouzeri* and the two-tiered Church of Saint Nicholoas. The undulating road N is our guide, initially tarmac then concrete then dirt, it rises and falls above the eastern shoreline of this mountainous, narrowing finger known as Gramvousa. Pass Balos Beach Hotel (the real Balos Beach is 10km (6 miles) distant!).

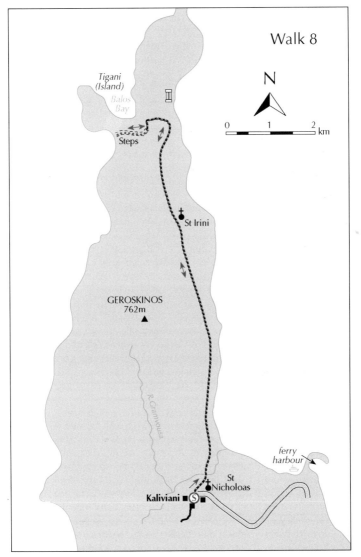

Ahead on our left, the rock- and scrub-clad flanks of Geroskinos, and over the blue waters of the gulf the great mass of Rodopou Peninsula. The peninsulas attract a variety of 63 in all seabirds, songbirds and birds of prey, and a further 29 species of nesting and migratory birds. Many colourful species of common and rare plants, such as sea chicory (*stamnagathi*), thyme, sage, prickly broom and the rare daisy anthemis, are found on Gramvousa. Of the resident animals and reptiles the most common is the ubiquitous goat – dozens line the track, particularly in the shaded vicinity of solitary Saint Irini (1), 1½ hours from Kaliviani.

When the end of the dirt track, now high above the shoreline, is in sight and Balos Col lies ahead, the track swings left past an incongruous *cantina* and small cruiser boat, some 100m (328ft) above sea level, alongside a spacious car park. With the central spine left and the rocky spearhead of Gramvousa right, the dirt pathway between rock and low scrub splits. Our route continues W, the narrow path to Vouxa (initially with red paint waymarks on the rocks) veers right, i.e. N, to Vouxa (Walk 9).

The relatively wide dirt track winds and drops W through a picturesque gully to join a zigzag stone stairway of 501 steps, of varying height and length, over-looking a site of extraordinary and unique beauty. Azure sea, golden sand in bays and beaches, islands of varying shapes that appear to float on the sea, Tigani ('pan and handle'), Pirates Bay, Pontikos ('little mouse') and surrounding islands (2) are beyond compare.

The return, if indeed you wish to, is via the outward route, providing extensive views of the hinterland and mountains of Kissamos, equally pleasing but totally different from those seen on the outward trek. ◄

To increase the pleasure and widen the experience of visiting the northern extremities of Gramvousa, why not utilise, in the summer season, the boat that sails daily from Trahilos to Imeri Gramvousa, stopping for a time to inspect the Venetian castle, and then to Balos Bay. A delightful cruise in one direction, a fine walk in the other.

Do not attempt the route west of Gramvousa's central spine, marked on both maps. It is highly exposed in places, having claimed lives and caused serious injury, due to an unstable 'moving' path of slippery, rounded stones underfoot.

Items of Interest

Tigani in Balos Bay

(1) **SMALL CHAPELS**. A feature throughout Greece, frequently seen close to the coastline, built by those who diced with death around these rocky shores and escaped, or those who lost a loved one at sea. Other chapels commemorate a family member who rose to an important position in life, or did great good for the community.

(2) BALOS, LAGOON AND SURROUNDING ISLANDS.

West and north of the peninsula's narrowing northern tip, small rocky relics of earthly upheavals were created in the mists of geological time, perhaps similar to the cataclysm at Phalasarna (Walks 13A and 13B). These small islands, together with the curved tip of the peninsula, form an ovoid similar to the rim around the caldera of Thira (Santorini). Could this have been the rim of an ancient and extinct volcano and the 'Ormos' Gramvousa the sunken caldera? Tigani, by the lagoon, translated is 'the pan and handle', very apt, for the connecting strip of land is its handle. Imeri Gramvousa carries the ruins of an imposing Venetian castle. The castle can be inspected, as can St George's Church on the islet, when the boat from Kastelli calls.

65

WALK 9

To Vouxa, Crete's Northwestern Extremity

Kaliviani, Balos Beach Hotel, Balos Col, Agrathos, Vouxa

Distance	32km (20¼ miles) there and back from Kaliviani on foot; 15km (9⅓ miles) there and back Balos Col to Vouxa
Height Gain	300m (984ft)
Start/Finish	Kaliviani – Saint Nicholaos Church, or Trahilos harbour (summer only)
Grade	4
Walking Time	10 hours
Maps	EFSTATHIADIS 1:79,000 CHANIA (with footpaths), ISBN 960 226 531 0
	harms IC verlag 1:100,000 Western Crete (includes E4) ISBN 3–927468–16–9
Accommodation	Kastelli and Kaliviani – hotels, apartments, rooms

Balos Col to Vouxa and back is a serious wilderness undertaking, requiring map and compass skills, as the peninsula perimeter presents sections of high exposure, and beyond Agnio there are no recognised paths through rock and scrub save random goat/sheep tracks. Whatever is underfoot fades into insignificance when compared to the surrounding seascapes and landscapes. Here are unique Cretan sights and sounds for 360°, from the isles below to the black bulk of Rodopou beyond the restless Gulf of Kissamos. Hasten slowly.

The Route

The initial outward journey to Balos Col would be either by ferryboat from Trahilos harbour (after inspecting the old Venetian castle on Imeri Gramvousa, disembark at

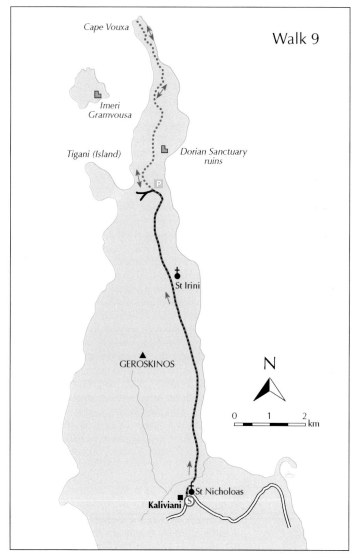

Tigani Bay and ascend the stepped zigzag, E, to emerge onto Balos Col with its car park and *cantina*), or by foot or car from Kaliviani. (See Walk 8 The Route, third paragraph, last sentence, for the footpath to Vouxa.)

From the *cantina* on the col walk towards the right corner of the cleared area and take the thin dirt pathway N. Underfoot the marked path (a red dot, sometimes ringed) twists and turns, rises and falls through rocks and small scrub on the initial stages of our 5km (3 mile) trek, mainly N and then NE, over undulating stone- and scrub-clad hillocks and large outcrops, 150m (492ft) to 250m (820ft) above sea level. A journey of challenges, crowned by seldom-seen views and accompanied by flowers, birds, goats, sheep and occasionally shy, half-wild donkeys.

Continue N through scrub and sage over several small cols. As the first is approached, note ahead, half-right, the archaeological site of Agnio, a Minoan ruin (1) surrounded by trees. Climb right over the shoulder ahead, rising over rounded rock to its highest point 253m (830ft) above sea level, known as Agarathos. Below, to the NW, it overlooks the angular isle of Imeri Gramvousa (2) with its Venetian castle and Saint Gorgios church. ◀

Ahead three stony hillocks confront, the centre one adorned with wind-worn sculptured rocks. The route to circumnavigate this triple barrier is to pass N, between the central and the right-hand hill, rising onto a narrowing plateau with a western rocky parapet 117m (384ft) above the restless sea. This northwestern extremity of Crete, Akrotiri Vouxa, offers unique northwest vistas of Agria Gramvousa (3), Imeri Gramvousa to the southwest, and Akrotiri Tigani to the south.

Return via the outward path to Balos Col, its *cantina* and high-and-dry boat. (For the return to Kaliviani see Walk 8).

Items of Interest

(1) **AGNIO**. One of several archaeological sites on the peninsula, this one is on the southern slopes, below the col, and contains the remains of a Dorian sanctuary, 1100–480BC.

The waymarked path is now behind us. The route ahead is basically with goat tracks through low scrub and sage over hillock and col, a way that is as individual as it is isolated on this deserted claw of rock.

(2) **IMERI GRAMVOUSA**. A triangular inshore isle, each flank 1km (²/₃ mile) or so in length, west of the crooked finger of Vouxa. The 1821 revolution ensured that one fortified stronghold remained in Cretan hands, i.e. the castle crowning Gramvousa Island. It fell to the Myrakis naval and military expedition of 1825 in a bloodless victory over the Turks, allowing Kissamos a brief period free from Turkish rule, but later that year Moustafa Pasha with 2000 troops returned to tighten the screw of oppression. However Imeri Gramvousa remained in Cretan hands – 3000 pairs of them! As so many were now confined on this tiny island the incumbents were driven to desperate measures to exist. They turned to piracy, hence the name Pirates Bay. A small chapel was built by the 'freebooters', and dedicated to the Virgin Mary, Cleftrina ('Protector of Pirates').

In 1827 the Greek government ordered a Scot, Sir Thomas Cochrane (acknowledged as 'the greatest man afloat'), Admiral of the Greek navy, to rid Crete of the pirate fleet. He failed, but not so the combined forces of Crete, France and England, which in 1828 sank the pirate fleet and gained entrance to the castle. In 1830 Crete petitioned Greece to return Gramvousa Island, but they refused, shipping the castle's armaments to mainland Greece. Later that year, as a pawn in the devious game of European politics, Crete, including Gramvousa Island, was returned to the Ottoman Empire!

(3) **AGRIA GRAMVOUSA** is an uninhabited, rocky, northwestern island extremity of Crete, 2km (1¼ miles) long and 500m wide, standing 40m (131ft) above the waters that wash the promontory of Vouxa. Its cliffs provide nesting sites for wild pigeons.

WALK 10

To Gramvousa's Pinnacle by
Church and Chapel

Kaliviani, Balos Beach Hotel, Saint Christos,
Geroskinos, Kaliviani

Distance	15km (9¼ miles)
Height Gain	760m (2492ft)
Start/Finish	Kaliviani, between church and *ouzeri*
Grade	4
Walking Time	6–7 hours
Maps	EFSTATHIADIS 1:79,000 CHANIA ISBN 960 226 5310
	harms IC verlag 1:100,000 Western Crete (includes E4)
	ISBN 3–927468–16–9
Accommodation	Kastelli and Kaliviani – Hotels, Apartments, Rooms

A direct ascent of Geroskinos from Kaliviani, initially via tarmac/dirt roads through vineyards and olive groves, ascending west and north on a zigzag to the chapel in a cave. Beyond it's a scramble up a narrow defile, then a wilderness ascent over rock and scrub to the coned grandstand summit of Geroskinos – 762m (2500ft). On a clear day, with an experienced eye, goat tracks, when linked, lead to the rocky summit. **Do not** attempt an ascent beyond the chapel in cloud or adverse weather.

The Route

Surrounded by vineyards, olive groves and increasing numbers of *thermokypra* (greenhouses), overlooking the Gulf of Kissamos and distant Rodopou, leave the village of Kaliviani at its northern end, passing between its distinctive church and *ouzeri*, first on a concrete slope, then tarmac, as olive groves and tamarisk trees line the flowered route N.

As the prominent bulk of Balos Beach Hotel hoves into view, look left and ahead for a zigzag dirt track probing the lower flanks of Geroskinos to a stratified outcrop above, our route for the day to church and chapel. Once past the hotel take the first left onto a winding dirt track, rising steadily for 250m (820ft). There are layers of tiered rock, studded with pebbles, as we pass through wire gates (leave them as you find them), eventually rounding the final bend that reveals church and chapel ahead. The lower one is secure beneath towering cliffs, and tiny Saint Christos (1) is glued within an overhang above.

A glance SE provides many spectacular land and seascapes – Kastelli, the Gulf of Rodopou and the Malathiros ranges to snow-capped Gingalos and the Lefka Ori (2). As the white walls of Saint Christos, the higher chapel, are approached, take care underfoot, as the stone-strewn paths are unstable and handholds are scarce.

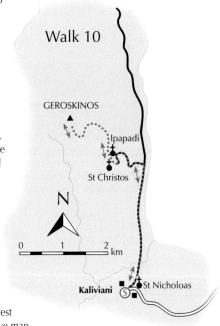

Now it is decision time, for ahead, once through the defile, there are no marked paths or dirt tracks, only a maze of thin goat tracks that require experience and rock-scrambling skills to reach the summit ridge. If Saint Christos is your goal, enjoy all it has to offer and return via your route of ascent. If Geroskinos summit calls, rest awhile by Saint Christos, have map,

Geroskinos'
southern summit

compass and altimeter at hand, and check water bottle and time. The route I pursued was as follows.

Two thin tracks spiral N from the fenced-in church to the gully above. Ascend NW to emerge onto the open eastern flanks. Continue ascending NW for 100m (328ft) then look back into the defile and line up the V of the gully with the elbow, i.e. angle, of Trahilos harbour walls to locate your exact position. This provides your point of return for a safe descent through the gully to Saint Christos. To mark this position I suggest a small pile of stones or a small branch from which to confirm your initial bearing through the V of the gully to Trahilos.

Continue ascending in a zigzag pattern, NW and SW, to the ascending N–S boulder-strewn ridge at a height of approximately 450m (1476ft). **The western side is severely exposed, so do not attempt to ascend N up its spine**. Drop 20–30m (66–98ft) below on the E side and ascend N with the spine to the head of a rock-strewn E–W gully below one of Geroskinos' coned summits. The final ascent is stony, via an intermittent path, but well worth the plod. The views span 360°, and those E are as magnificent as they are far-seeing, including distant Psiloritis (2).

Return to the base of the summit cone and descend initially SE, i.e. 120°–140°, through a shallow gully (its left side, i.e. N, rocky and higher), continuing over rock- and scrub-scattered slopes, between 110°–120°, ESE, to the head of the defile above Saint Christos. This descent, not waymarked, is on a series of narrow zigzags, within the limits of the given compass bearings, over the eastern flanks of Geroskinos. The final scrambling descent through the defile to the church is set at 110°, and the final steps to the coast road are via our outward route.

Once past the hotel walk S to the line of tamarisk trees on the right and a wiremesh fence left. At the southern end of the fence turn left, i.e. E, on an overgrown track to the shoreline site of a storm battered Lebanese freighter (removed 2003) (3). After inspecting the site walk S on the dirt track, taking the first right to pass several tomato *thermokypra* (greenhouses) (4). When our outward road is met turn left for Kaliviani.

Items of Interest

(1) **SAINT CHRISTOS**. Marked by a conspicuous white cross above, this tiny chapel clings to the cliff face offering, in addition to spiritual guidance, a far-reaching panorama to the south and east.

Trig point on Geroskinos' summit

(2) **LEFKA ORI and PSILORITIS**. Both provide a spectacular backdrop for long-range photographs from the heights of Geroskinos. The Lefka Ori, or White Mountains, south of Chania, are 48km (30 miles) as the crow flies, so called because they can retain snow into July, and in their northern gullies all year. Their highest peaks comfortably top 2200m (7220ft). Timios Stavros, at 2456m (8058ft) Crete's highest peak within the Psiloritis massif, 112km (70 miles) east-southeast, tops the Lefka Ori's Pachnes by a mere 3m (10ft).

(3) **SHIPWRECK SITE**. Here lay the rusting, wave-battered remains of a Lebanese freighter out of Beirut, carrying animal feed bound for Kastelli in 1981. She steamed into the bay, winds light northwest, and lay at anchor overnight with engine problems, intending to dock the following day. Through the night the winds shifted north, increasing to storm force, and although the engineer attempted to repair the engine it was decided to sail her into harbour. The engine had little power, the north wind had too much, and at 10am, 10 January 1981, she was blown inshore and cast upon the rocks below Kaliviani.

(4) *THERMOKYPRA*. These greenhouses, invariably large and plastic clad, with a controlled trickle feed of water and nutrients installed, produce much-sought-after Cretan tomatoes, peppers and cucumbers. Lorry loads leave daily for the hungry markets of Athens, via the ferryboats from Souda Bay, Chania.

WALK 11

*An Adventurous Ascent of
Geroskinos' Eastern Slopes*

*Kaliviani, Balos Beach Hotel, Geroskinos Gully,
Saint Christos, Balos Beach Hotel, Kaliviani*

Distance	10km (6¼ miles)
Height Gain	300m (984ft)
Start/Finish	Kaliviani, between church and *ouzeri*
Grade	4
Walking Time	4 hours
Maps	EFSTATHIADIS 1:79,000 CHANIA ISBN 960 226 5310
	harms IC verlag 1:100,000 Western Crete (includes E4)
	ISBN 3–927468–16–9
Accommodation	Kaliviani – hotels, apartments, rooms

A journey of contrasting environments requires from the walker mountain experience and in-built navigational and map-reading ability as **the route is not waymarked**. A scenic shoreline stroll on dirt and stone tracks leads to a challenging stone and rock scramble of 270m (886ft) up a narrow gully on the riven east face of Geroskinos. Emerge onto the rippling, stone- and scrub-clad eastern upper flanks of the Gramvousa Peninsula for an undulating adventure south and east to the twin churches, before a zigzag dirt and stone descent to Balos Beach Hotel and Kaliviani.

The Route

Start from the imposing, towered church of Saint Nicholoas, at the north end of Kaliviani. Walk N on the olive- and vineyard-lined Balos tarmac/concrete, and later stones/dirt, road overlooking the blue waters of the Gulf of Kissamos. Contrary to the roadside notice the Balos Beach Hotel is further than the '1km' stated. More important is that our hillside gully/gorge in the eastern flanks of Geroskinos is 3.5km (1¼ miles) north from Kaliviani church.

From the hotel continue N with the rocky shoreline track, passing a prominent conical rock on the right while ahead, overlooking the Balos track, an equally conspicuous shoulder of rock juts eastwards, dominating the northern rim of our narrow gully of ascent. Entry left to the gully is a few metres before an ever-open gateway and small trackside animal pen. Ascend W, i.e. left, via a thin dirt path that rises over rock- and tree-scattered ground, then through ground-hugging scrub and later stone/boulder fields that carpet this narrow, steep, rock and cliff-fast gully (¾hr to this point). ◀

This ascent is for walkers experienced in steep ascents and rock scrambles through uncharted mountain gullies.

Wind-bent bushes point W, as if to signal the route that provides a choice of goat tracks, ribbons of scree or small loose rocks. From this point I suggest you divide the route into short sections – firstly up to a large cave on the right with a tree at its entrance, above an easy ascent by goat tracks through scrub, or by stone-covered ways on the gorge floor left of centre.

From the cave the way is W with stone chutes, zigzagging slightly, a degree or so either side of W. Sage and ground-hugging scrub claw at the ankles as the cave is left behind and we continue to our next target – a solitary conifer leaning towards the N face of the narrowing gully. With rock and scrub on the left,

Walk 11

† St Irini

▲ GEROSKINOS

Geroskinos gully

† Ipapadi

† St Christos

N

0 1 2 km

† St Nicholoas
S ■ **Kaliviani**

Narrowing rocky gully

ascend W, approaching the marker tree from the right-hand half of the gully by crossing a stone chute zigzagging between rock and scrub on a red-earth pathway. The tree is a pleasing resting place from which to access the now visible exit route via the head (a small corrie) of the ravine.

The choice is either to follow close to, or with, the dried watercourse on the left as we look left, or to ascend half-right onto the shelf on the right-hand cliff. I took the latter, as the extremely narrow watercourse appeared to be restricted by several large boulders – passable but not too easy. **The scramble onto the right-hand (N) shelf requires concentration.** Hasten slowly but surely to the exit from the gully by bearing left, with initially a dirt and mainly scrub-free goat track passing S. (Hill fires of 2003 cleared much of the scrub.)

Once clear of the gully emerge S onto Geroskinos' rocky and sterile eastern slopes, setting a bearing to contour S. A glance NW reveals the angular stone summits of Geroskinos on the skyline, while ahead, i.e. W, rises its half-hidden, domed southerly summit. It's an easy wildwalk, a degree or so W of S, over stone and dried earth, with our gully's protruding northern bastion now behind. A total contrast to the confines of the gorge are the wide-open, far-seeing views S and E of Profitas Ilias, Kastelli, Trahilos, Rodopou, Gulf of Kastelli and the Lefka Ori.

Continue contouring S on the same bearing, crossing several small, shallow, descending gullies spearing E from the summit ridge, to meet a more prominent gully, also identified by four 'caps' of flat, rounded rock astride its northern ridge. Its southern side is pitted with a variety of south-facing caves – a moonscape walk?

With the caves now behind and Kaliviani and Trahilos prominent below, set the compass on a bearing of 10° W of S for the next 300m, looking left over the rocky rim below for sightings of the Balos Beach Hotel and a narrow cleft in the rock. Beyond, an inverted dirt pathway leads E of S to the visible slash in the rim below and ahead, allowing access to the two churches in and on the rocks. This descent is not by waymarked paths, but over the wilderness eastern flanks of Geroskinos, much favoured by hares (1). The scrambling descent through the defile to the two churches (2) and (2A) is set at 110°. The final steps to the road are via the zigzagging, descending dirt vehicle track, to join, with a right turn, the outward route just N of Balos Beach Hotel. Return S to hospitable Kaliviani.

Items of Interest

(1) **WILD HARES**. With blue-grey fur, these agile and curious rock-hoppers are much given to rearing up on their hind legs to see what's going on.

(2) **SAINT CHRISTOS**. Above a steep and unstable pathway this tiny chapel is inset into the cliff wall and marked above by a prominent cross. Is it a sign of the times that this chapel of Christos has to be encased within a bolted, metal-meshed fence?

(2A) **IPAPADI** Restored in recent years, this T-shaped church is now tidy and cool, fenced and walled.

WALK 12

A Scenic Journey to Tilifos
Monasterie below Geroskinos

Kaliviani, Azogiras, Tilifos Monasterie, Saint
Gorgios, Azogiras, Donkey Track to Kaliviani

Distance	7.5km (4¾ miles)
Height Gain	200m (660ft)
Start/Finish	Kaliviani
Grade	2
Walking Time	3½ hours
Maps	EFSTATHIADIS 1:79,000 CHANIA ISBN 960 226 5310
	harms IC verlag 1:100,000 Western Crete (includes E4) ISBN 3–927468–16–9
Accommodation	Kaliviani – hotels, apartments, rooms

A walk through productive olive groves and vineyards to/from the mountain fastness that cradles Tilifos Monastery, discovering the remains of Saint Gorgios in the area known as Habatha. A walk generous in scenery, wildlife, ancient times, solitude and surprise.

The Route

Start from colourful Kaliviani, proceeding S past the Kaliviani hotel, rising with the road alongside a series of white or pastel-shaded houses as far as a sharp right-hand fork. Ascend right by a single tree, on a series of zigzags, between thriving olive groves W and WSW to the rural village of Azogiras.

At Azogiras turn right at the T-junction, then swing left and turn right (here note a directional notice written in Greek, 'Monasterie ΤΥΛΙΦΟΥ' (Tilifos)), again passing houses where every one seems to be a farmhouse, with chickens, turkeys, sheep, goats and noisy dogs. Leave

Azogiras via a wide track descending towards the rock and ridge of the southern aspect of shapely Geroskinos. To the right limestone outcrops, indented and caved, stand high above a

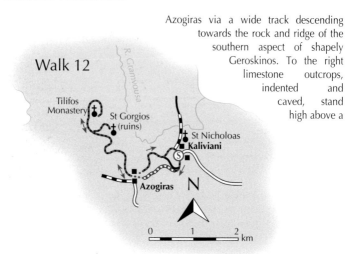

Walk 12

R. Gramvousa

Tilifos Monastery

St Gorgios † (ruins)

† St Nicholoas
Kaliviani

S

Azogiras N

0 1 2 km

narrow gully running into the Gulf of Kissamos below Kaliviani.

With dirt and stone underfoot, descend to cross a ford, home to a horde of vocal frogs, before ascending the water-loving-oleander-fringed track W and NW. Surrounds are rocky, gorse clad and domed, undulating and ascending. Flowers line the way for most of this part of the journey, which has the great ridges of Geroskinos rock in its sights. Walk W and N. On the left note the descending valley of olive green from Platanos to Kaliviani; note also the sharp ascending bends in the track, concreted to prevent wheel spin and subsequent erosion. Ahead are full-frontal views of the western face of Geroskinos massif as our goal for the day, Tilifos Monastery, comes into view.

The track, broad and red, runs between fields of barley and thin oats. At this point look behind to scan the dominant dome of Profitas Ilias. Once identified, continue looking left, i.e. E, along the jagged ridge to a conical hill at the end of a flat ridge, which is the ridge

The green oasis of Tilifos Monastery

and summit of ancient Polyrinia, crowned by the Church of 99 Saints (Walk 17).

Pass through the only gate along the way (leave as found). The road/track now begins to swing left, with a carob tree alongside, as we round the dome that obscures the craggy southern aspect of Geroskinos. Descend a little to swing left and arrive at a T-junction, swinging with the concrete track E and N to approach the monastery. At the second fork veer right to the fenced enclosure containing three buildings – cells, chapel and a new pantiled east wall. The most interesting approach is to drop right before the wooden double doors, descending to tiered and stepped wells and water troughs on the southern perimeter of Tilifos, in company with a cluster of majestic plane trees.

Rise with the steps to the SW corner of the chapel where a wire gate allows entrance beyond a well. Inspect, enjoy and leave as found. Note the clapped-out bell dated 1916 and the central well on a slabbed area (1958).

For an extension of the monastery walk, continue on a dirt and stone track towards a clutch of caved and tree-bound outcrops far below the exposed rock of Geroskinos. (While researching this area north of Tilifos, there was a fenced area contained feeding troughs and what appeared to be a 'hippies' decrepit blue-and-red VW van.)

*The remains of
Saint Gorgios*

Return to pass the monastery via its northern side and join the outward track. At the fork ahead swing left, passing the remains of a series of monks' cells or shelters for animals. Beyond, note on the left amidst the scrub and rock a white cement slab on the ground, 7m x 4m, beside a small, crumbling ancient shell of a temple or chapel with a one-time arched roof (1). After careful inspection retrace your steps to the outward path back to Azogiras, a stretch seen to advantage in late spring or early May (2).

From the central T-junction, i.e. the second met on our outward journey, walk SSE to the prominent two-storey house at the SE side of the village. Pass the building on its right-hand side, SSE, by a colourful patch of geraniums, to walk on a thin path alongside an olive grove towards a fenced animal shed. Before this, veer left through an olive grove on a trampled dirt trod N to swing right and descend slightly. Leave the olive grove as derelict stone walling is met, turning half-left to join a pathway between an old wall and a wiremesh fence, NE on an old donkey track of limestone slabs. Continue NE, above the ravine on the left, until a large house (blue shutters) to the right is spotted and olive groves are met. Turn right with the track/pathway SE to just below the house. Pass the house (one of four) onto a dirt track left, i.e. N, towards a single house ahead. Before the house swing left across a walled flat area of olives to descend, guided by blue dots on stones and trees, to meet a blue arrowhead. At this point turn right between a walled terrace and wiremesh fence – there are fine views N to Geroskinos and the Gulf of Kissamos, with Kaliviani immediately below.

Descend with the zigzagged waymarked path into the welcoming heart of Kaliviani by the Church of St Nicholaos.

Items of Interest

(1) **SAINT GORGIOS**, said to be 400 to 500 years old, is possibly from the late Byzantine period of the Venetian occupation, 12th–17th centuries. Plans are in hand to restore and reconstruct the ruin, and hopefully its Byzantine paintings.

(2) **BIRDS OF PREY**. Of the many species of raptors encountered in Crete, two of the most prevalent and interesting can be seen and/or heard on this walk. The *cucko-vaya* owl (cuckoo owl) is rarely seen, but this tiny 'boinking' bird is frequently heard as darkness falls, as are the responding calls of fellow owls, filling the evening air with a barrage of 'boinks'. The peregrine falcon (*Falco peregrinus*), also known as 'the king of birds', is perhaps the most graceful, dexterous and lethal of all the raptors. This elegant killer can be seen hunting along the route from Azogiras.

WALKS 13A AND 13B

An Eagle's-eye View of

Phalasarna Bay and Cape Koutri

Kavoussi, Falasarna, Phalasarna 'Harbour',
Cape Koutri, Azogiras, Kaliviani

Distance	A) 10km (6¼ miles), B) 13.5km (8½ miles)
Height Gain	250m (820ft)
Start/Finish	Kavoussi (by Platanos)/ A) Falasarna, or B) Kaliviani
Grade	A) 2, B) 3
Walking Time	A) 3 hours, B) 6 hours
Maps	EFSTATHIADIS 1:79,000, CHANIA ISBN 960 226 531 0
	harms IC verlag 1:100,000 Western Crete
	ISBN 3–927468–16–9
Accommodation	Platanos, Falasarna and Kaliviani – hotels, apartments, rooms

A delightful scenic walk, via dirt pathways or tracks, by sandy shore and mountain ridge, with but one testing ascent. Crowned by (A) the archaeological wonder of Phalasarna's 'high and dry' ancient harbour, surrounded by dramatic rocky capes and shorelines, before an olive-flanked, panoramic return to Falasarna or, alternatively (B) for the enthusiast, to the east coast of Gramvousa Peninsula at colourful Kaliviani.

The Route

Start from the triple junction, between Platanos and Kavoussi (1), posted 'Falassarna–Sfinari–Kissamos'. Our route is via the dirt road N with the chapel on the left. Vineyards line the flowering banks, and a turquoise sea with a scatter of islets in Livadi Bay washes the sandy shore far below. Ahead to the north the bulk of Geroskinos points to the heavens and on our right sections of omnipresent Rodopou dominate.

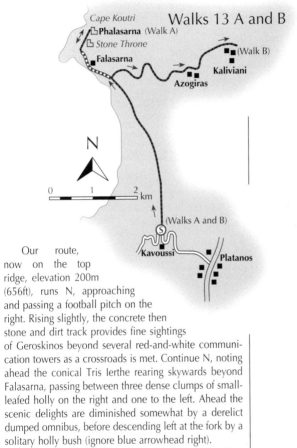

Walks 13 A and B

Our route, now on the top ridge, elevation 200m (656ft), runs N, approaching and passing a football pitch on the right. Rising slightly, the concrete then stone and dirt track provides fine sightings of Geroskinos beyond several red-and-white communication towers as a crossroads is met. Continue N, noting ahead the conical Tris Ierthe rearing skywards beyond Falasarna, passing between three dense clumps of small-leafed holly on the right and one to the left. Ahead the scenic delights are diminished somewhat by a derelict dumped omnibus, before descending left at the fork by a solitary holly bush (ignore blue arrowhead right).

The next 3.25km (2 miles), gradually descending NNW with only one fork (we take the left), are a visual delight through olive groves allowing fine views of an azure sea – a carpet of dancing sunlight – extensive sandy beaches and a canvas of intriguing, coned rock formations beyond the scattered village of Falasarna (2),

85

The stone throne of Phalasarna

in addition to the not so visually appealing plastic green-house settlement below. Falasarna is a curious mix of tourist rooms, apartments and tavernas, served by a daily bus to and from Kastelli, and the original agricultural village that produces the finest Myzithra cheese in Kissamos. The descending track finally emerges into the centre of Falasarna at the 'Beach Apartments', adjacent to a car park and bus stop, by the OTE telephone.

Pleasing as the village and surrounds are it is the Phalasarna of antiquity, 1km (⅔ mile) to the NW that has unique appeal. Leave the car park NW, and with the wide track pass on the left, just before the kiosk leading to the site of Phalasarna, the dominant stone throne (3) of Phalasarna.

The excavation site of the ancient Minoan one-time harbour, canal and city of Phalasarna (4), overlooked by Cape Koutri's finely profiled peaks, sits today on dry land 100m from the shoreline that rose 6.5m (21ft) above sea level, the result of a cataclysmic upheaval. As antiquarians record, Phalasarna is unique.

Explore and absorb this remarkable Minoan city port, admire the masonry skills of the fourth and first centuries BC, ascend Koutri ridge, before returning to the car park and OTE telephone in Falasarna, the end of Walk 13A.

Walk 13B continues, from the car park and OTE telephone, E on a concrete footpath alongside a plastic tomato house. Ascending right on the stony way, above adjacent buildings, we meet a track left marking the start of an old zigzag rising to the col above, leading to Azogiras.

Take this track left for 30m or so to a bend left, (ahead the track becomes overgrown, making passage difficult and slow). Leave by stepping right onto a thin path rising E sharply but safely, with occasional footholds, up the steep hillside for 10 minutes or so to join the original zigzag track. Continue ascending, slightly overgrown in places, to the col, pausing to admire extensive views of Falasarna and the coastline. Once over the col descend, this time on a relatively new dirt and stone track, with extensive views of Geroskinos,

Ancient Phalasarna below Cape Koutri

the Gulf of Kissamos and the dark mass of Rodopou Peninsula.

As height is lost, either keep a close watch on the left side of the dirt road for a thin path (marked by a pile of six stones in 2003) leading half-left through scanty scrub to a fence and marker pole, or continue with the broad track to where it swings right. Turn left onto a twintrack on the upper tier of terracing. 15m along this way a large waymarked stone (a red T) indicates the fence-side path some 70m N.

Descend E with the fence to where the path splits. Our path veers right between one tree right and two trees left into and through the olive groves. After a short distance S swing left onto a higher tier of well-tended groves, walking E along a compacted trod to emerge via a tangle of ancient and decrepit animal shelters before a tarmac farm road and six snarling dogs, fortunately tethered. ▶

Circumnavigate both dogs and farmhouse, descending to the friendly village of Azogiras set in a sea of olives (5). At the second T-junction turn right then first left onto a descending road/track into Kaliviani.

Note several of the olive trunks passed are waymarked with blue paint, unfortunately only on the east side, i.e. the reverse side when walking east!

Items of Interest
(1) **KAVOUSSI**. It is worth a short stroll to see its Venetian buildings and St John's Byzantine church.

(2) **FALASARNA**. The initial 'F', as opposed to the historic 'Ph', distinguishes the modern settlement from the historic city port. Catering for today's tourist trade, it is a scatter of apartments, rooms, hotels, tavernas, bars and beach furniture. Its most appealing assets are kilometres of gently sloping soft sands, warm sea and proximity to ancient Phalasarna.

(3) **STONE THRONE OF PHALASARNA**. Cut from solid rock, it sits by a road junction, providing the inquisitive with questions, but few answers. Who was it for? Why is it so rough hewn and fashioned with too low a seat and too high arm rests?

(4) **MINOAN PHALASARNA**. Named after a pre-Hellenic nymph and archaeologically the third most important city within Kissamos, being the enclosed (by canal) port for its inland sister city of Polyrinia (Walk 17). Protected by an impregnable fort close to fertile lands, it prospered as an international trading centre, as well as a military/naval base that was not averse to piracy.

Showing great independence, its soldiers were for hire and it minted its own coins (imprinted '.Φ.Α. – Phalasarna'). Excavations reveal circular and square towers, sinks for washing clay, fortification walls and, on the summit ridge of Koutri, an acropolis littered with the debris of ancient structures, including fourth and third century 'cisterns'. Its nemesis came with two major earthquakes, 66AD and 635AD, tilting Western Crete 6.5m (21ft) above sea level. Gargantuan waves buried harbour, canal and parts of the city beneath layers of silt.

(5) **OLIVE TREES**. Approximately 70% of cultivated land within Kissamos nurtures the olive, known in ancient times as 'the golden tree'. Gathering olives takes place as winter approaches. Huge, close-meshed nets are spread beneath the trees to catch the fallen 'gold', which is taken to the olive press then stored in jars.

WALK 14

A Seat on Manna,

Grandstand of Profitas Ilias

*South of Platanos (on road to Zachariana), Vrises,
Profitas Ilias, Manna, Maganistra Gorge, West of
Zachariana, E4 to Platanos*

Distance	11.25km (7 miles)
Height Gain	590m (1936ft)
Start/Finish	Platanos – south end
Grade	4
Walking Time	6 hours
Maps	EFSTATHIADIS 1:79,000, CHANIA ISBN 960 226 531 0
	harms IC verlag 1:100,000 Western Crete
	ISBN 3–927468–16–9
Accommodation	Platanos – hotels, apartments, rooms

A rewarding circular walk for experienced, well-equipped walkers to one of the finest grandstands in Western Crete. The ascent of Manna is challenging although never exposed. Exposure however is present on the western and southern rim of the summit from which classic views of Kissamos Gulf and Gramvousa and Rodopou peninsulas are revealed. This mountain walk encompasses a fascinating high land area followed by a descent on the western rim of Maganistra Gorge, where I learnt 'goat speak' (Walk 25).

The Route

Leave the southern extremity of Platanos, via the Sfinari road, for 750m to reach the T-junction of the Zachariana–Lousakies road running left, i.e. E. Turn left for 300m to the first dirt track branching right, i.e. S. Here is the real start of this adventure, waymarked by the black-and-yellow pole and ◇ of the ◁E4▷ trail (1). This waymark is holed (as are many others) by rifle bullets – up to 0.33mm! (a national pastime in Crete).

Walk S between olive groves to be greeted with the highlight of the day, as the clinging cloud moves on to reveal the great rock massif of Profitas Ilias (2), in particular the revered westerly peak of Manna, 890m (2920ft). Continue S, initially with the olive-lined track, gazing directly up to and into the great slash between pointed Manna and the crags of its neighbour. The rising zigzag track with lengthy straights provides fine views of our route, i.e. straight up the gully between the two mountains. It may look testing, and it certainly is, but don't be discouraged, for the rewards are high.

For 1.75km (1 mile) the track rises and falls to reach the foot of the gully, marked by two large plane trees (*platanea*) at the base of a stony, dried-out watercourse, 35 minutes from the initial ◁E4▷ sign. Begin the ascent between these two trees. The gully ascent description is not a step-by-step guide for all grades of walker, it is a series of suggestions for the experienced, i.e. look at the gully ahead and above and pick what for you is the most suitable, overall, route to the col above. I have found it advantageous to break the ascent into shorter sections, and when the first goal is reached it provides a closer look at the next section, and so on, to the col above.

The overall SSW ascent of 450m (1476ft) covers approximately 1km (²/₃ mile) via safe goat/sheep tracks alongside watercourses. When using hands to aid ascent, always test the bush, plant or rock for stability before applying your full weight. Animal tracks are easier to ascend than the stones – at times unstable – in a dried-up stream.

Initially the watercourse provides the route, later abandoned to swing left utilising animal tracks through scrub, stone and finally outcrop rock, to reach the col approximately 1hr 15mins from between the two plane trees.

Once on the col the wide dirt track leads right i.e. W, for a short distance to a parking area (of all things!) below the domed summit of Manna. From the car park a narrow path zigzags W to the fascinating summit rocks and wall-encircled Chapel of Profitas Ilias on Manna. Here are views encompassing 360° of sea, summits and sculptured rock – Kastelli, Kaliviani, the valley from Lousakies to Kastelli, Falasarna, Sfinari Bay and Sfinari, Livadi, the Gulf of Kissamos, Gramvousa and Rodopou peninsulas and E, S and SE to the summits and high ridges of the Lefka Ori. In a word, the entire area that is Kissamos and Selinos, after a journey of 1¾ hours from the initial ◁E4▷ sign.

South to Manna on Profitas Ilias

93

Caution – the west and south rim of the rock- and scrub-clad summit, above the somewhat neglected chapel and its surrounding shelter wall, is 'extreme' and should be treated with great caution. From this western 'seat of the gods', where cloud can cover at the drop of a hat, we looked down on soaring vultures and wheeling golden eagles.

The descent, S, E and N, is a sedate and safe affair on these scenic balconies of Kissamos. A wilderness of contorted rock, sudden valleys and gorges make this hike from Manna's car park a journey of new experiences and views along a gradual zigzag of dirt and stone tracks. A route that wriggles through ethereal outcrops of light-grey rock, continuing S only to suddenly wheel around, as if on an acute angled track, to journey N and then E. Passing goat pastures of colourful scrub, turn sharp left as the mountains ahead appear to plunge into the upper ravine of Maganistra Gorge (3), between the eastern peaks of Profitas Ilias and to the east the bulk of Kouvara.

With a communications mast to our right the red soil track undulates E. Ahead, domed summits rise from the valleys far below as we now travel S over the col to swing left, i.e. NE, surrounded by green scrub and white rock, through this unique landscape. Now we are looking into a steep-sided valley with a twisting road SE, running from the southerly head of Maganistra Gorge, met after a zigzag descent. Once on the rim of the gorge, reached by turning left at the junction, look into its upper reaches, tree clad and scrub covered, as we descend with the mountains of Volakes and Kouvara shoring up the west and east walls of Maganistra. Our track N passes a dilapidated farm on the west side of the gorge, before swinging W to meet the towering red-and-white communications mast of girders and dishes.

Turn right, i.e. N, at the mast for a twisting, turning descent to the pleasing village of Zachariana. If you plan to stay in Zachariana or neighbouring Lousakies **it is advisable to check the accommodation availability.** If not, turn left on the waymarked, tarmac ◁E4▷ road to return to the E4 starting point and Platanos.

Items of Interest

(1) **EUROPEAN LONG DISTANCE PATH**. The ◁E4▷ long distance path, the fourth in Europe, starts in Spain and enters Crete at Kastelli. From here it journeys through the scenic regions of Kissamos and Selinos. It leaves the area at Anidri Gorge (Walk 38) to continue east through the Lefka Ori, the heights of Psiloritis, Lassithi Plateau and the Dikti Mountains, before continuing east to terminate at the archaeological site of Zakros above Zakros Bay – Crete's eastern extremity – a testing hike of approximately 320km (200 miles). Several walks within this guide tread sections of the E4.

(2) **PROFITAS ILIAS**. A collection of summits of which Manna ('Mother'), crowned by the small, walled Chapel of Profit Ilias, is the highest and most prominent, providing views covering the west and northwest shoreline of Kissamos. Given a clear sky, it is possible to see the distant islands of Kythera and Antikythera, and also the summit of Taygetos in the southern Peloponnese.

(3) **MAGANISTRA GORGE**. A deep, V-shaped chasm, the gorge runs north to south for approximately 5km (3 miles), splitting the mountain ranges of Profitas Ilias to the west and Kouvara to the east. Access to its centre is difficult and not recommended. The best way to view the gorge is from the western rim, i.e. the track detailed in the walk. This atmospheric gorge, choked in places with bushes and scrub, is a favourite of wild pigeons. The area beyond its southern end is known as Pateriana, an historic but now deserted neighbourhood that was used at the time of the Turkish occupation as a secure meeting place by Cretan chieftains. It was here also that the Cretan 'Syrtos' dance was first performed on the occasion of a marriage.

CHAPTER 2

The Scenic Heart of Kissamos

South from the main coastal road and old village road that travels west from Nopigia, passing Drapanias, Kaloudiana and Kastelli to Platanos, rises the bulk of the Principality of Kissamos. Bounded on its southern and western flanks by the Libyan and Mediterranean seas, the region covers 522 sq km (202 sq miles), with an approximate population of 19,400. It has, apart from in the height of summer, escaped the annual deluge of beach tourism.

THE AREA

With nearly 50% classed as mountainous and 18% taken over as fertile agricultural/arborial land, the area presents a picturesque landscape of varied shades of green in which, nestled in valley floors or clinging to surrounding hillsides, white-walled, flower-bedecked villages lie, each with a tale to tell and a reason to visit. Although it is mountainous, fine walks can be found, particularly on the high ridges and in the many gorges. It also enjoys a mild Mediterranean climate of dry, warm summers and reduced spring and autumn rainfall.

With its varied terrain and unique history there is much to please and challenge the walker. As the area is extensive, and the walker may not have transport, the 20 walks that explore this diverse heartland have been arranged in progressive groups around an accommodation base. The accommodation base gives access to the start and finish of the walk (although linear walks may require wheeled transport to return to the accommodation). Suggested bases are Topolia/Katsomatados for Walks 15–24, Elos for Walks 25–29, and Kefali for Walks 30–34.

From twisting gorge and breezy col to mountain tops and coastal cliffs, the walks of Chapter 2 provide unique insights into this westerly region of Crete, and also its turbulent history. They range from a short stroll of 1.5–2km (1–1¼ miles) inspecting Saint Sophia's cliff-face cave, to a 14km (8½ mile) trek 'To Milia and Beyond'. Gorges are explored, and mountains ascended, including the region's highest, Dikeos 1184m (3885ft), with its wheeling vultures and soaring eagles. A revered monastery is visited, along with the azure waters of the lagoon and islands of Elafonisos. Ridges, valleys, abandoned villages and olive presses and today's vineyards are all met along the way, while in spring carpets of flowers add interest and pleasure.

THE WALKS

Walk 15, entitled 'High Expectations and a Little Sadness', starts from Voulgaro then journeys through groves of olives and fruits, passing charismatic Makronas Memorial, to ascend the narrow Portopharago Gorge leading to Saint Farangi and the friendly villages of middle and upper Malathiros. **Walk 16** starts and finishes at the high ridge settlement of Topolia, a journey of constant change and far-seeing vistas. **Walk 17** winds through the Sirikari/Sprikari Gorge to the ancient Dorian city of Polyrinia, a gorge walk overflowing with flora and fauna, while **Walk 18** trips through Manolis Motakis' olive groves to visit

the spacious cave and revered chapel of Saint Sophia. **Walk 19** stretches legs and lungs as it rises from Katsomatados to restored Milia before an undulating return, via Kalathenes and Keramariano Gorge, to Katsomatados. **Walk 20** prowls from Katsomatados to the head of Keramariano Gorge, descending the gorge for a switchback scenic return via Tsourouniana and Trapeza. The circular 'King of Kastelos' **Walk 21** is a near neighbour of Walk 20, replacing the gorge walk with a rocky ascent of Kastelos. **Walk 22** is a circular from Katsomatados, sampling the views from the col above Sassalos, then ascending the rocky, far-seeing

Elos to Agios Dikeos (Walk 25)

summit of Leventies above the Topolia Gorge. **Walk 23** is the longest scenically varied walk from Katsomatados, ascending through chestnut groves, descending into the narrow Athanassios Gorge, strolling through olive groves and *mouri* to inspect Latziana's Byzantine Monastery of Saint Barbara, before passing the Topolia Gorge and climbing to hillside Topolia and thence to Katsomatados. **Walk 24**, the last walk from a Katsomatados/ Topolia base, provides a pleasant hike after a good lunch at Costis' Platania Taverna in Vlatos.

Walk 25, the first walk to use Elos as the accommodation base, ascends the 'Olympus' of Kissamos. Regardless of its height, Dikeos is a pleasant and rewarding mountain hike (look out for soaring vultures). **Walk 26** is a delightful rural stroll on the Inahorion foothills of the Tiflos valley – a colourful journey enhanced by four charming villages and Crete's oldest plane tree. **Walk 27**, with a mysterious crater, a donkey track and a seat in the 'gods', is a scenic gem. **Walk 28** is a colourful journey to Sassalos that will test your navigation

skills but never your stamina, while colourful **Walk 29** descends west, in company with olives and chestnut trees, from the interesting village church of Louhia to Perivolia, and beyond to its neighbouring village of Vathi.

Kefali, overlooking the Stomio Valley, provides an accommodation base for the remainder of this chapter's walks. **Walk 30** visits the ailing Byzantine church of Saint Paraskevi on its lofty perch, a journey that reveals this extensive valley, its surrounding mountains and gorges. **Walk 31** takes us from one side of the Stomio Valley to the mountainous enclave of Tzitzifa, recommended for seekers of solitude. **Walk 32**, the Plokamiana loop, strolls through a flower-strewn gully, peers into Skotini Gorge, and returns through old olive groves to Plokamiana. **Walk 33** is a circular, visiting five villages gracing the hillside and valley floor within Stomio Valley, and finally **Walk 34** travels the old way from charismatic Monasterie Chrisoskalitissis, with its 'golden step', through the coastal wilderness, to the unique bay, lagoon and surrounding islands of Elafonisos.

WALK 15

High Expectations and a Little Sadness

*Voulgaro, Makronas Memorial, Portopharago
Gorge, Mesi and Apano Malathiros
(Martyrs Memorial Church)*

Distance	6.5km (4 miles) to Malathiros
Height Gain	250m (825ft)
Start/Finish	Voulgaro, 8km (5 miles) SE from Kastelli on the Topolia road/Malathiros at the Church of Saint George
Grade	3
Walking Time	4 hours to Malathiros, 4½ hours to Sassalos
Maps	Wanderkarte KRETA Chania, 1:79,000
	harms IC verlag 1:100,000 Western Crete ISBN 3–927468–16–9
Accommodation	Rooms and refreshment in Voulgaro

A walk through groves of olives and fruit alongside the Anilios river to the charismatic Makronas Memorial, and beyond to the picturesque side gorge of Portopharago, an off-shoot of the spectacular Halasses Gorge. In places this walk requires respect, plus map and trekking skills, but in return river and gorge reward the walker's efforts with a display of nature's wild and wonderful beauty.

The Route

From Voulgaro's main square (1), overlooked by its imposing church, leave SE via a descending minor road, lined and scented with olives, wisteria, orchids and fuschia, to cross River Tiflos alongside an engineering workshop. At the first junction swing right, an arrow pointing SE, leading onto a dirt track to a cemetery. Continue past the cemetery through a narrow cleft and olive groves on a flat dirt track, keeping the river in sight and sound on the right.

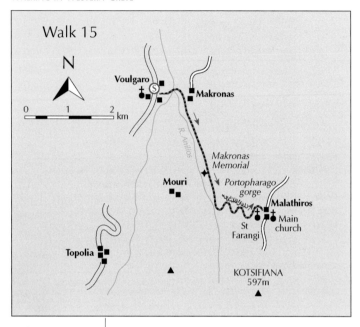

Walk 15

N

0   1   2
|_____|_____| km

Voulgaro

Makronas

R. Anilios

Makronas
Memorial

Mouri

Portopharago
gorge

Malathiros

Main
church

St
Farangi

Topolia

KOTSIFIANA
597m

Seven hundred and fifty metres beyond the cemetery an old ivy-and-vegetation-clad arched bridge leads right over the Anilios. Inspect it if you wish, but continue S on this fine path for a further 500m to the charismatic and moving memorial dedicated to the martyrs of nearby Makronas (2). The river and entire gorge surrounding the memorial, clothed by a colourful mix of varied vegetation, fully deserve their 'Site of Exceptional Natural Beauty' accolade.

From this place of remembrance continue a degree SSE of S with the dirt track to come face to face with one of Kissamos' natural geological wonders, the constricted cleft of Halasses Gorge (3). Narrow and deep, it is considered impassable for much of the year, except in September and October when the river has all but dried up. A further hazard can be 'falling rock' dislodged by goats on the cliffs above.

Our route takes the scenic, in places steep, ascent via the Portopharago Gorge side branch, leading to two of the three villages of Malathiros above. Approaching the mouth of Halasses, our narrowing pathway meets the river ahead, where a wooden waymark 'Μαλαθμβο' (Malathiros) directs us E, via a well-crafted, albeit narrow, ascending zigzag, up to and beyond a spectacular, pencil-thin waterfall plunging over a water-worn cleft of Jurassic sandstone. Beyond the waterfall a network of paths ascend E, crossing the tree- and scrub-lined descending stream several times, eventually emerging from the trickling watercourse and stone-slabbed donkey track onto a dirt twintrack, alongside which stands a large concrete water tank, left. On the right, opposite the tank, two prominent brown-and-yellow noticeboards in Greek announce, 'Council of Mithimnos and the State Water Suppliers have received money from the European Community' and 'Route for Nature-lovers, Sassalos–Makronas'.

Turn right, pass the water tank, and a metre past the noticeboards veer right, leaving the track via a narrow, distinct path/trod leading to the now visible church

The Memorial to the Makronas martyrs

101

The northern jaws of the Halasses Gorge

ahead, Saint Farangi, 'Church of the Gorge', surrounded by vigorous olives. The gorge has now metamorphosed into a widening, but still steep, fertile valley of well-tended vegetable and fruit gardens. Leave the church, ascending E with the clearly visible donkey track, through stepped and terraced gardens, E, S and E again for 10–15 minutes to emerge into the middle village of Malathiros, via a farm, onto a rising concrete track left, i.e. N and W, with extensive views, to reach the main road to Apano Malathiros. Turn right, i.e. S, for a short stroll to the clearly visible village overlooked by its impressive twin-towered Byzantine main church and adjacent war memorial, site of a unique commemoration, held every year on the final Sunday of August to honour the fallen.

Items of Interest

(1) **VOULGARO**. In 961AD the modern-day village was populated by the Bulgarian troops of Nikiphoros Fokas. This fighting force rid Crete of the first Turkish occupation, creating the second Byzantine period. Later, during the 17th–19th centuries, occupying Turks settled in Makronas by Voulgaro.

(2) **THE MARTYRS OF MAKRONAS**. On the fateful morning of 28 August 1944, before the departure of occupying German forces, 60 Cretan males, aged 13 to 66, were taken from Makronas village and massacred at the site of today's memorial. Each man is remembered by name and age on surrounding brass plates. Central to this emotive memorial, between track and river, are three simple, geometric concrete pillars. One bears text in Greek, the central one a sculptured rising Cretan head. The third pillar displays a poignant sculpture of the local *pappa* (priest) – who by quick thinking and a great deal of luck was the sole survivor of the shooting and the pistol-to-the-head – rising from the dead. Lush vegetation and tinkling waters provide a fitting surround for the memorial, overlooked by the heights of Mouri, a large church, and serenaded by the cooing of doves and croaking of many frogs.

(3) **HALASSES GORGE**. A north–south gorge of two branches 2km (1¼ miles) in length, split asunder when the earth was young as if by the wrath of Cretan gods. The Anilios, having risen below Milones, runs by Sassalos, hurrying into the gorge at its southern end before flushing through an underground tunnel at the centre of the gorge. By Voulgaro the Anilios joins the Tiflos (from Agios Dikeos, Elos and Topolia Gorge) to flow north into the Gulf of Kissamos. Not so many years ago, when water levels were higher, there were pools within the gorge where turtles and eels bred.

WALK 16

Tsourouniana to Topolia's West Ridge

Topolia, Tsourouniana, Trapeza,
Topolia's Ridge, Topolia

Distance	8.45km (5¼ miles)
Height Gain	300m (984ft)
Start/Finish	Topolia on the Kastelli–Elos road
Grade	2
Walking Time	3½ hours
Maps	EFSTATHIADIS 1:79,000 CHANIA ISBN 960 226 531 0
	harms IC verlag 1:100,000 Western Crete
	ISBN 3–927468–16–9
Accommodation	Rooms and refreshments in Topolia and Katsomatados

The mountain settlement of Topolia's constricted, tortuous main street provides the start of the walk, with variety as its theme. Vistas constantly change, as does the route underfoot. Never too tiring, every ascent is richly rewarded. Don't be discouraged when the route utilises stretches of tarmac road – they are quiet country roads with pleasing views.

The Route

High above the Topolia Gorge clings Topolia, through which the main road from Kastelli to Elos squeezes. Start from the northern end of the highest zigzag of the main street before it descends to a church below. Do not follow this descending road, but ascend the Aikirgiannis and Kalathenes road N, soon to meet and pass under the first delight of the day, a giant canopy of oak (1) spanning the road. Beyond, rise to and over the col of Topolia's western ridgewest.

Here are striking views, W of the surrounds of Kalathenes and the sugarloaf of Profitas Ilias, as the road divides. The left fork goes to Tsourouniana, the right leads to Aikirgiannis and Kalathenes (ignore dirt track left, i.e. S). Follow the new tarmac road for 1.6km (1 mile) to Tsourouniana (shown as a footpath on the recommended maps) to the half-hidden village, on two levels, colourful, charming, friendly and well worth a browse either now or later on the return leg.

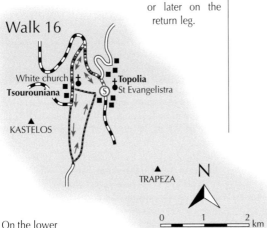

On the lower level at its southern extremity there is a sharp U-bend, beyond the white church, that connects with an ancient, ascending, stone-laid donkey track S, liable to double as a stream in places after heavy rain. Take this interesting route S, rising through olive groves and fruit trees, for approximately 1km (⅔ mile) to connect with what was a dirt road, now a tarmac road. Turn left at the junction, walking S for a short distance to turn left again, this time ascending E for the upland plateau of Trapeza and the ridge above Topolia.

Approaches to the southern end of the ridge, on a winding road, provide not only a fine walkway but also varying vistas. S and SE note the lonely wilderness and

Topolia's giant oak

pinnacles of Trapeza, high above Topolia Gorge (2) and the Cave of Saint Sophia. As the ridge is reached and the ridge path leads N we are within sight of an extensive panorama that includes an immediate eagle's-eye view into Topolia (3) on the hillside below. To the north lies the entire Tiflos Valley from Topolia, via Voulgaro, to Kaloudiana and the blue waters of the Gulf of Kissamos, flanked by Gramvousa and Rodopou, with the hills and ridges of Rokka to the right (E) and the ancient city and gorge of Polyrinia and the domed mass of Profitas Ilias to the left (NW and W).

Continue N along this scenic way to meet, on the left, a winding track ascending from the white church of Tsourouniana. Turn left to the picturesque village and its musical stream, which can now if time permits be explored further, before the return to Topolia over the col and past the great oak.

Items of Interest

(1) **THE TOPOLIA OAK**. Said to be Crete's largest and oldest, this magnificent tree is best seen in spring, viewed from its northern side and framed by cypress trees, when its emerging leaves are a soft green and its sturdy trunk surrounded by a carpet of colourful spring flowers.

(2) **TOPOLIA GORGE**. 1.5km (approximately 1 mile) long, its colourful, crumbling rocky sides pockmarked with small caves and inhabited by luxuriant flora and a variety of birds and small animals, the gorge rises 300m (984ft) above the 5–50m wide floor, eroded by the surging River Tiflos. Folklore recounts that the Minoan goddess Vritomartis, together with fairies and the giant Talos, who apparently was a fan of fairy music, lived in or visited the gorge.

While researching this guide (2002–4) sections of both east and west walls of this mighty gorge were weakened further. A few years previously an enraged, in-spate River Tiflos dislocated sections of the gorge wall, and subsequent deluges eventually dislodged great boulders of rock onto the road and into the floor of the gorge, closing it indefinitely.

(3) **TOPOLIA**. Within Cretan time Topolia is a modern village. The Great Fire of August 2002, a disaster probably started by August's extreme heat, petered out metres short of Topolia township. Olive groves, fruit trees, stately poplars and resinated conifers were charred to a cinder. Scrub, including *Ebenus cretica*, Crete's most attractive spring-blooming bush, was also torched below and above the road leading through the Topolia tunnel (one of only two throughout Crete). Miraculously, as the flames approached the perimeter buildings and a church, the direction of the wind fanning the flames changed.

WALK 17

Through Sirikari Gorge to Polyrinia

Sirikari, Sirikari Gorge, through
Koustogiannides, Polyrinia

Distance	5.6km (3½ miles), x 2 if return to Sirikari
Height Loss	82m (269ft)
Start/Finish	Sirikari/Polyrinia
Grade	2
Walking Time	2½ hours
Maps	EFSTATHIADIS 1:79,000 CHANIA ISBN 960 226 531 0
	harms IC verlag 1:100,000 Western Crete
	ISBN 3–927468–16–9
Accommodation	Rooms and refreshment in Sirikari

The Sirikari Gorge is one of the most scenic and benign gorges in Western Crete, containing a pleasing selection of chestnut groves, plane trees, wild olives, locust trees and holly, in addition to colourful ground-hugging plants and scrub. Birds are in profusion, from soaring raptors to tiny song-birds in the valley floor alongside the watercourse. Little wonder it has been declared a national park. At its northern end unique Polyrinia provides much for the student of ancient Cretan history.

The Route

Our adventure starts from Saint Konstandinos above Sirikari. From the church gates cross the road to a mesh gate leading onto a thin, descending, steep-in-places zigzag path W and NW, through scrub and olive trees, into the southern jaws of this famous gorge. Hasten slowly should the earth underfoot be wet, eventually to arrive onto a wide trackway through a wiremesh gateway. Note the red waymark on the trackside pole close to the gate if you are returning by foot to the starting point. Turn right to pass by old farmhouse buildings, one of which has a classic clay oven.

From these buildings the gorge walk proper begins, N and NNE, passing the lower western flanks of dominant Sfakokefala on the right. Now free from close-growing olives the scenery is set as we approach the river, and beneath narrowing walls of stark, bare rock and the now dry, tree-shaded, boulder-strewn riverbed, we join a path coming in from the left from Sineniana.

From here the northbound pathway passes through the narrowing gorge on the east side of the riverbed, alongside beds of head-high sage, beneath varying shades of green platania, castanea and acer, and by fallen rocks as large as houses. Before a stone-built terrace – a welcome viewpoint and refreshment stop – note the concrete water tanks by the side of the path. Overhead, screeching, 2-metre wingspan eagles soar effortlessly above the sheer rock faces of the high cliffs of Kouvara 713m (2339ft) and its towering neighbours, while bird-song bounces off cliff faces. The N end of the trek opens from the narrow V ahead, providing the first glimpse of the white or pastel-walled flat-roofed houses of Polyrinia clinging to the heights of the Polyrinia ridge ahead.

*North from Sirikari
into the Sirikari Gorge*

Meet and cross a classic, arched stone packhorse bridge (1) over the riverbed beyond which waymarks – red dots on rocks and trees and yellow and blue arrowheads – on the ever-winding dirt and stone track lead us N, steadily ascending beyond a water-pumping/generating station, to meet a tarmac road rising to Kato and Apano Polyrinia.

After joining the tarmac, leave it to ascend and then descend left, i.e. on a grass and dirt twintrack NW, crossing the creek below the southern flanks of Polyrinia village and ridge to the north. The final metres to this unique, charismatic village zigzag, passing an old water fountain where village clothes are still washed today, to the three arches at the centre of the village (2).

From this point a concrete, stone and dirt zigzag ascends to the dominant Church of 99 Saints on the ridge above this ancient Dorian city, a church whose walls are inscribed with many letters and texts. Note the ruins of a Venetian castle above, and the prehistoric remains of an ancient Dorian city gouged into the soft rock of the ridge, (with sleeping quarters, water tanks, etc.).

Should you wish to return via the outward route, there are even more stunning views when walking S. Note the dramatic turreted hills ahead through the gorge, but do not miss the red paint dots on rock and tree, particularly the one on the trackside pole marking the final ascent and exit (just beyond the old farm buildings with the clay oven) to Saint Konstandinos.

Items of Interest

(1) **PACKHORSE BRIDGE**. As to its age, I cannot say; its purpose, I would suggest, was to assist passage inland through the gorge to and from Polyrinia, the capital. Its design bears a remarkable resemblance to the old pack-horse bridges found in the North York Moors, in the vicinity of Tynedale and Hadrian's Roman Wall.

(2) **POLYRINIA**. In the third and second centuries BC this classical city (later state), 7km (4⅓ miles) south of Kastelli, was a dominant player in the commercial, artistic and military (particularly against Knossos) development of Crete. Many suggest Phalasarna (Walk 13A and B) was the port of Western Crete, but this is doubted by Hellenic scholars, as at least 20km (12½ miles) separates the two. Kastelli, a mere 7km (4⅓ miles) to the north, had in Mavros Molos (Walk 6) a functional harbour as far back as the 12th century BC.

Polyrinia flourished under the Romans. It quickly grasped the advantages and cooperated, while other states resisted and rebelled. Under the Roman overlords Caligula, Trajan and particularly Hadrian (of Roman Wall fame), Polyrinia prospered. It minted and circulated its own coins, and had a main street and tunnels to a water reservoir built under Roman supervision. The Polyrinian statue of the Roman General Metellus demonstrates the city's appreciation of its benefactors.

WALK 18

Saint Sophia's Cave

Katsomatados, Cave and Chapel of
Saint Sophia, Katsomatados

Distance	1.6km (1 mile)
Height Gain	100m (328ft)
Start/Finish	Panorama Taverna, Katsomatados, on Elos road
Grade	1
Walking Time	30–40 mins
Maps	EFSTATHIADIS 1:79,000 CHANIA ISBN 960 226 531 0
Accommodation	Rooms and refreshment at the Panorama Taverna

A gentle incline through an olive grove, with fine views of the hills surrounding the upper reaches of Topolia Gorge as the flower-flanked pathway reveals the arched entrance of Saint Sophia's Cave, high in the western wall of Topolia Gorge. The final short ascent joins a stepped walkway from the highway below.

The Route

Opposite the terrace of the Panorama Taverna, by the corner of a house, a signpost indicates our pathway at the head of a short flight of steps. A dirt path, made and maintained by Manolis Motakis of the Panorama Taverna, winds N through olive trees. Never claustrophobic, views of the cliffs that flank the Topolia Gorge (1) and the hills above are revealed to the east. Tree cover gives way to scrub and flowers as the pathway winds past several boulders before revealing spectacular sightings of the triangular opening of Saint Sophia's Cave (2), below the flat ridge known as Saint Sophia's Doma ('roof'), and the pinnacle of Trulos ('round tower'). Our path now meets and ascends the zigzag steps leading to the yawning cavern (3) (4) (5) above.

A tiny chapel stands within the entrance arch, topped by a bell. The vast interior is filled with a mass of ever-changing stalactites and stalagmites, fashioned drop by drop since time began from water-washed limestone. The cave is home to myriads of startled bats, swifts, swallows and pigeons. Lime-loving plants cling to the rounded rock and mosquitoes dance in shafts of sunlight. Take care when exploring the dark interior of the cave, as boulders and rock underfoot are wet and slippery.

Return to the Panorama Tavern via our colourful outward path.

Items of Interest

(1) **TOPOLIA GORGE**. In 2002 and 2004 the Topolia Gorge, after winters of constant deluges, was closed to the walking public, as were the tunnel and roadway for a short time to motorised traffic. Gorge walls collapsed, eroded by the swollen River Tiflos (known as 'the Blind River') and torrential rain. Roadways collapsed as their foundations were weakened. Hopefully one day the gorge will be reopened for pedestrians and the weakened walls strengthened.

(2) **SAINT SOPHIA**. A slight misnomer, as the name of this mother of three daughters means in Ancient Greek 'the Wisdom or Mind of God'.

(3) **THE CAVE**. 20m (65½ft) high, 70m (229½ft) in diameter and 100m (328ft) above the Topolia highway, the cave is held in great respect, not just in Crete but throughout the Greek Orthodox Church. Home to the recently refashioned shrine of Saint Sophia, Easter service is held within the cave on the morning of Easter Monday.

113

Entrance to and Chapel of Saint Sophia

(4) **FOUND IN THE CAVE**. Neolithic shards, a previously unknown insect now christened *Spermophora topolia* and an icon of Saint Sophia, brought from Constantinople by Cretan soldiers who fought there, have all been found in the cave. Before 1204, during the Turkish occupation of Crete, the Military Governor demanded the heads of two Cretan leaders who were hiding in the cave. This was not possible, as the cave was strongly defended, so he captured the sons and other relations of the two leaders and threatened death to all if the sons did not behead their fathers and present the heads to the Turks in Chania. The sons naturally refused, but the fathers insisted, and after much soul searching it came to pass. The families were then freed and united. In the 1800s stonemasons were building a new chapel and levelling the floor of the cave when they discovered two headless bodies. Today the two bodies lie in state beneath the priest's table.

(5) **EASTER IN KISSAMOS**. The Day of Days, and there is, even to a stranger to the Greek Orthodox Church, something in the air, an expectation, an outpouring of fervour and worship as Easter Day approaches. It is as if Christmas and Scotland's Hogmanay are rolled into one, and then some. Days before, Greek TV transmits a constant flow of footage of a population migrating to the villages of their birth – roads blocked, ferries overflowing and not a seat available on domestic flights.

WALK 19

To Milia and Beyond

*Katsomatados, Milia, Kalathenes,
Keramariano Gorge, Katsomatados*

Distance	14km (8¾ miles)
Height Gain	450m (1476ft)
Start/Finish	Panorama Taverna, Katsomatados, 2km S from Topolia
Grade	3
Walking Time	5 hours
Maps	EFSTATHIADIS 1:79,000 CHANIA ISBN 960 226 531 0
	harms IC verlag 1:100,000 Western Crete ISBN 3–927468–16–9
Accommodation	Panorama Taverna, Katsomatados

A circular hill and valley walk offering diverse views, ranging from the Lefka Ori (White Mountains) to Kissamos' coastal plain. Underfoot a variety of waymarked, signposted paths, dirt roads, farm tracks and quiet country lanes, it is best walked in April and early May, when Cretan flowers burst forth, from tiny violets to giant lilies, and the air vibrates with busy bees.

The Route

Fifty metres S from the Panorama Tavern's roadside drinking-water tap, a sign on the right indicates a marked ascending pathway, made and maintained by Manolis of the Panorama, zigzagging W through trees and scrub. Beyond the second gate (leave as found) our pathway joins a wider way ascending right. The legs may complain, not so the eyes. Views increase as the gradient eases past a solitary scrubby tree on the left. Continue to a dirt roadway contouring the hillside ahead. Once reached turn right, following the dirt road N, with occasional signs to Milia, for a short distance. It descends W,

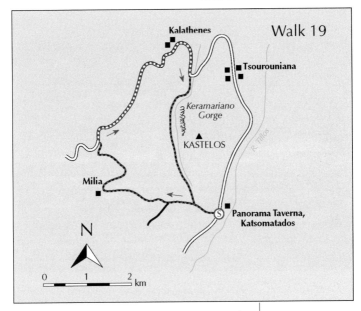

to and through a copse of sweet chestnut trees, with a small chapel and farmhouse close by. Continue with the signposted dirt road ascending W on the slopes of the side valley where the restored village of Milia (1) lies partially hidden. Colourful wild flowers and varying greens of trees accompany us as we drop into Milia's signposted car park. Take time to browse around peaceful Milia – refreshments are available.

Leave the car park via the footpath signposted 'Sirikari Path', ascending NNE then NW, through a profusion of broom, leading onto a small plateau at the head of the valley. The villages of Sirikari and Miheliana lie below to the west, and Sirikari Gorge (Walk 17) can be seen wriggling N to the ancient city of Polyrinia. Take care underfoot – some rocks are hidden and occasionally unstable. Depart N from the plateau via a descending stone-capped rough track which is joined right, i.e. N. Descent on this 'coggly' track provides breathtaking

*The traditional
settlement of Milia*

views N. As the rocky road swings left the surface improves, joining a small country road that descends in picturesque sweeps NNE to floral Kalathenes (2), with its Venetian rotunda at Upper Kalathenes.

This friendly, two-tiered village descends via a sharp bend to eventually peter out, before yet another acute bend at the floor of the valley. Leave the tarmac road right, before it straddles Keramari stream, below the village of Aikirgiannis, on a dirt track as it arcs S, flanked by flourishing fruit trees and ever-present olive groves, into the narrowing jaws of Keramariano Gorge (3).

Between olives and oranges, the track is surrounded by lush undergrowth and flanked ahead by five peaks. As the right ridge slopes into the ravine, note the silhouetted stone figure of An Cailleach ('Old Crone or Witch') of Milia stirring her cauldron. Ignore the left turn by swinging W and then S over a side stream, then, ignoring the path right, carry on S to squeeze between a sugarloaf summit, Kastelos (Walk 21), left, and the 'Old Witch' and other outcrops right. Ascend S with the track, crossing several streams, through this 'Garden of Eden' – home to melodious birds including seasonal migrants, and a mix of stoats, hares, and the ubiquitous goat, and an all-embracing solitude.

The stony track, sometimes gentle sometimes testing, is gated as it ascends, providing reverse sightings of Rodopou and Gramvousa peninsulas. At a small shrine, left, the track swings right over the stream, soon to be crossed again alongside a clutch of platania (4). Pass by the tiny chapel of Saint Georgios and meet the farm buildings and sweet chestnut grove (5), seen on the outward journey, at the foot of Milia Valley. Once through the gated wire fence turn left, i.e. E, rising with the broad track, flanked with *koomaros* (6), joining the Milia road to the T-junction of the outward journey above Katsomatados. The journey down, below the heights of Trapeza, is via our outward path to Katsomatados.

Items of Interest

(1) **MILIA**. An old, abandoned, derelict village, the traditional settlement of 'Milies' was restored in a joint venture between Greek (Cretan) restoration specialists and finance from Germany. The village however is not a working village – it is entirely for the tourist. A similar post-war gesture by the Bavarian Ministry of Agriculture reforested an area near Vlatos.

(2) **KALATHENES**, 300m (984ft) above sea level. Smart, well-maintained dwellings and gardens are the hallmark of modern Kalathenes. There are also eight old mills, a Venetian villa rotunda and an arched Venetian building.

(3) **KERAMARIANO/KERAMARIA GORGE**. The name originates from the ceramics – pots and tiles – produced within the gorge in times gone by. Fertile and productive, unlike its many rocky, dramatic cousins, such as the unstable Topolia and the narrow cleft of the Halasses, it is a paradise for resident and migratory birds, and flora and fauna.

(4) **PLATANIA**. Water-loving plane trees need continuous supplies to thrive. Their presence is a reliable indicator to the Cretan farmer of a water source. Well-watered trees grow for centuries. The oldest, reputed to be 1400 years old, thrives in the garden paradise of Vlatos.

(5) **SWEET CHESTNUT**. *Castanea sativa* is a graceful tree with a shapely green leaf, found in the vicinity of running water. The sweet chestnut thrives around Elos and Katsomatados. Years ago, invited to the farmhouse to take coffee with the family, from grandmother to grandchildren, for all take part in harvesting, we were given a few choice nuts. Out came my Swiss knife to remove the leathery shell. 'Not that way', laughed the matriach, 'this way', as she crunched the entire nut between toothless gums!

(6) ***KOOMAROS***. A native shrub thriving on the hills of Kissamos, its flowers, favoured by bees, produce a good, although somewhat bitter, honey. It is from the berries that *raki,* the 'spirit' of Crete is produced.

(6A) **BEES**. Beware not so much the bee, but a species of Cretan wasp that invades beehives. Rejection by the bee makes wasps very angry and frustrated.

WALK 20

High, Wide and Handsome

Katsomatados, Keramariano Gorge,
Tsourouniana, Trapeza, Katsomatados

Distance	9km (5½ miles)
Height Gain	400m (1312ft)
Start/Finish	Katsomatados/Katsomatados
Grade	3
Walking Time	4 hours
Maps	EFSTATHIADIS 1:79,000 CHANIA ISBN 960 226 531 0
	harms IC verlag 1:100,000 Western Crete
	ISBN 3–927468–16–9
Accommodation	Katsomatados

A circular, hill and gorge walk, rich in solitude and indigenous wildlife, that challenges and delights. Underfoot dirt and stone paths, sections of tarmacked country road, bulldozed dirt tracks, and an old ridgeway track overlooking the 'half-way house' of Tsourouniana and extensive Tiflos Valley.

The Route

From the Panorama Tavern's roadside drinking-water tap, walk S for 50m to 'Manolis' Path', a waymarked zigzag ascending W, initially through trees and colourful scrub. Beyond the second wire-and-wood gate (leave gates as you find) the path joins a wider, and in places steeper, bulldozed way ascending right. Views increase as height is gained – now we can gaze into the Topolia Gorge – and as the gradient eases, pass a solitary scrubby tree left, revealing ahead a dirt roadway contouring the hillside. At the T-junction, with numerous directional markers, take the 'Milia' route, but not before scanning SE beyond the Tiflos Valley to the distant snow-capped Lefka Ori.

Our dirt road, with occasional signs to Milia, leads N for a short distance then W (note the relatively new bulldozed/tarmac road on the right ascending N – our return route from Topolia Ridge) to approach a cluster of sweet chestnut trees, with a farmhouse ahead and a small white chapel visible to the right. With the chapel as a waymark, turn right through the wire-fence gate following the track N, past white Saint Georgios, leading into the benign gorge called Keramariano (1).

Flourishing flora colour the jagged skyline as we continue N, on a stone and dirt track that crosses the musical stream twice, initially alongside a clump of platania, to meet a roadside shrine on our right. Continue N with the stony track as the gorge walls gradually narrow and descend, flanked by one sugarloaf summit known as Kastelos (Walk 21), and small side valleys where solitude and nature are in harmony. Even the gates we pass through are perfectly crafted, unlike the 'wire-and-tree-branch' models met elsewhere.

Approaching the lower northern end of the gorge, pass by irrigation channels between extensive olive groves and fruit orchards. Our path veers N over an incoming stream, then right, i.e. E, for the final sweep N on the dirt track through yet more olives, oranges and

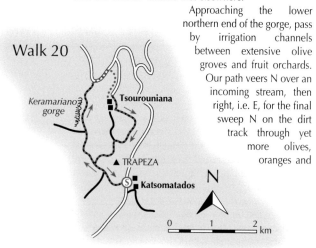

Through Keramariano Gorge

undergrowth, finally emerging onto the U-bend of the Kalathenes–Aikirgiannis road. Turn right, crossing the Keramari waterway, and ascend NE with the roadway, towards Aikirgiannis, for approximately 500m. Bypass the village right, SSE, on a rising grassy twintrack, to emerge onto the halfway point of the new road from Topolia Col, leading right – S – into Tsourouniana (a pleasing although scattered village that invites inspection). Leave E from the white church via an ascending concrete path through olives to the ridgeway above.

At the T-junction on the ridge turn right, i.e. S, to follow the ridge path high above the houses of Topolia clinging to the slopes of the northern entrance of Topolia Gorge below. Views N, E and W, of peninsulas, a gulf, mountains, gorges and valleys, from this 450m (1476ft) high ridgeway, are breathtaking, and great fun if you have a map handy. Take care not to stray off the pathway left, where one or two points of high exposure lurk. Soon the track swings right and leaves the ridgeway for a gentle stroll W to a T-junction. Turn left, i.e. S, leading onto a tarmacked road, ascending and winding through the pimpled wilderness of Trapeza, or right, i.e. N, via an old donkey trail descending to Tsourouniana. We take the wild way left, i.e. S.

The solitary road winds S and SW, rising with a series of acute zigzags through rock- and scrub-clad summits and pinnacles above Saint Sophia's Doma ('roof') (Walk 16) and the pinnacle of Trulos. Emerging above the head of the Keramariano Gorge, look out for encircling birds of prey before joining the outward track on the Katsomatados–Milia route. Turn half-left and left again, some 50m ahead at the signposted T-junction, descending SE via the outward route to Katsomatados.

Items of Interest

(1) **KERAMARIANO GORGE**. Blessed by an ample supply of spring water, this gorge, where once were manufactured a variety of ceramics, is today a 'Garden of Eden'. An orchard of fruit trees, flowers and many flourishing olive groves, in times past it nurtured a wide range of vegetables. It also provides a home and a staging post for many resident and migratory birds, including the Harrier eagle and other raptors.

WALK 21

'I'm the King of Kastelos'

*Katsomatados, Milia Track (Fingerpost 'Kastelos'),
Tsourouniana, Katsomatados*

Distance	8km (5 miles)
Height Gain	300m (984ft)
Start/Finish	Katsomatados/Katsomatados
Grade	3
Walking Time	3½ hours
Maps	EFSTATHIADIS 1:79,000 CHANIA ISBN 960 226 531 0
	harms IC verlag 1:100,000 Western Crete
	ISBN 3–927468–16–9
Accommodation	Katsomatados – rooms and refreshment

This walk of great beauty, far-seeing views, challenge, satisfaction and solitude, will appeal to all lovers of the great outdoors. You need not ascend the rock-clad summit slopes of Kastelos should you not wish – it's a hill that looks as good from below the summit as it does from the summit.

The Route

From the Panorama Tavern's roadside drinking-water tap, walk S for 50m to 'Manolis' Path', commencing on the right, a waymarked zigzag ascending W, initially through trees and colourful scrub. Beyond the second wire-and-wood gate the path joins a wider, in places steeper, bulldozed way ascending right. Views increase as height is gained, and as the gradient eases pass by a solitary scrubby tree on the left – ahead a dirt roadway contours the hillside. At the T-junction, with its numerous directional markers, take the 'Milia' route to the right, i.e. N.

As the way descends a tarmac road joins from the north. Ignore this recent highroad (utilised on the return) and continue on the sloping zigzag dirt track – past a solitary tree and the sign 'Milia'. A few metres beyond the first U-bend we meet a wiremesh gate marked by an arrowhead waymark – 'Kastelos' – directing us right into the northern quadrant. Pass through the wiremesh gate onto a prominent pathway that can be seen rising N below a series of rocky bastions on its right and a supporting wall, in places, on its left. A gated path, varying from 2m to 1m in width, well waymarked and in places overdone by yellow or orange splodges and red arrowheads, rises between sage (1) and broom with pleasing views left, i.e. W, to the Milia community above the southern end of the Keramariano Gorge by the Church of Saint Georgios. **While admiring the views it is advisable to stop, as underfoot are stones that are unstable and could turn an ankle, for as you progress N the pathway becomes steeper.** Ascent is by rocky steps, and even more colourful as Kastelos Col draws closer.

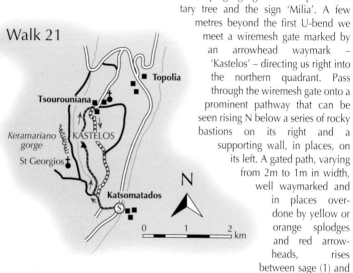

Walk 21

■ Topolia

Tsourouniana ■

Keramariano gorge

KASTELOS

St Georgios ✝

Katsomatados

Ⓢ ■■

N

0   1   2 km

The ascending pathway swings right, i.e. NNE, onto the colourful col below Kastelos, now on our left. Broom lines the dirt trod, and as we pass through ground-hugging scrub our yellow-waymarked way swings left, and with the splodges ascends, between 350°–360° N, the accessible, stone-strewn flanks of Kastelos. As ascent continues the pitted rocks tend to increase in size. Red arrowhead waymarks appear in places to give the climber a choice of routes. **I use the** word 'climber' in its true sense, for as the summit approaches ascent grows steeper and stonier, frequently requiring hands as well as feet. Wire fences also impede progress, making the final metres to the twin summits difficult. **If in any doubt do not attempt to go further on this prominent but small hill.**

From the flanks of the coned summit the views are breathtaking in all directions, in particular the peninsulas of Rodopou and Gramvousa, the Gulf of Kissamos and its hinterland. **Descent to the col below requires care, in places more so than when ascending.**

From the two yellow marker stones on the col, that marked our point of ascent of Kastelos, amid a sea of swaying broom, walk left, i.e. N, on a track with a fence on its right hand but no waymarks. Ahead is a gate with a huge rock on its left side. Here swing half-right of the dirt and stone track looking directly into Kastelli Bay. Note the twin cones above Polyrinia (Walk 17) half-left

Start of the Kastelos walk

as we pass a lone trackside tree to descend, past a large gully on the left, between olive groves and later vineyards (2), on a rock-slabbed donkey track. This section surpasses many in Western Crete for near and far scenic views (3).

Swing NE to descend via a well-used track, through olive groves, that provides sightings on the left of Kalathenes and beyond to Gramvousa. The now tarmacked road that leads left via several U-bends into the scattered, floral village of Tsourouniana is now met.

On the lower level of the village, at its southern extremity, is a sharp U-bend beyond the white church (4) that connects with an ancient, ascending, stone-laid donkey track S, liable to double as a stream after heavy rain. Take this interesting route S, rising gradually through olive groves and fruit trees for approximately 1km (⅔ mile) to connect with a tarmac road. Turn left at the junction, walking S to the foot of a series of steeply ascending zigzags and U-bends winding SSW through the wilderness of Trapeza. Look out for encircling birds of prey before joining the outward track on the Katsomatados–Milia route by veering half-left then left again, some 50m ahead, at the signposted T-junction, descending SE on the outward route to Katsomatados.

Items of Interest

(1) **SAGE**. Renowned in Greece from ancient times for its therapeutic properties, sage is particularly good for the stomach. it is mentioned by medical masters such as Dioscourides (On Medical Matters) and Hippocrates on diet. In Crete, a sage infusion is used as a stomach relaxant and a disinfectant for the mouth and gullet. It also reduces the secretion of sweat, saliva and milk. Up to 40 or 50 years ago a profitable enterprise for Kissamos was the harvesting and marketing of sage.

(2) **VINES AND VINEYARDS**. The well-tended, sun-kissed vines of Kissamos are reputed to produce grapes of exceptional strength. Did not the god Dionysos, 'taste their sweet and wild fruit'? And did not the son of Zeus

Kastelos from Tsourouniana vineyards

declare that 'two or three glasses of the red wine of Kissamos are essential for good health'?

(3) **OUTSTANDING VIEWS**. Gazing back to the vineyards and beyond, from where we came, to Kastelos rising bell-like to its narrowing, domed summit, above our descending track backed by Psilo Kefali 903m (2963ft) towering above the enclave of Milia.

(4) **CHURCH TOWERS AND TILES**. Some churches display red-tiled roofs and red-painted domes, while others are blue. Is it a visual reminder of the 'Great' or 'Greek' schism of 1054, when the Greek Church separated from the Latin? Apparently not, for according to my Cretan adviser on matters ecclesiastic, the answer is simply that the colour displayed is the colour that is visually pleasing to the *pappa* (priest) and the majority of his congregation!

WALK 22

Leventies – the Character of Kissamos

Katsomatados, Saint Demitrios, Sassalos Col, Leventies, Katsomatados

Distance	9.25km (5¾ miles)
Height Gain	425m (1394ft)
Start/Finish	Katsomatados, Panorama Taverna, 2.5km (1½ miles) south from Topolia
Grade	2–3
Walking Time	3½ hours
Maps	EFSTATHIADIS 1:79,000 CHANIA ISBN 960 226 531 0
Accommodation	Rooms and refreshments in Katsomatados

One of Kissamos' pleasing and relaxed ascents, with extensive and enjoyable panoramic views from the mountain's summit, whose sheer, naked western flank provides Topolia Gorge's eastern bastion. Our ascent is via the 'back door', on wide dirt tracks winding through olive and chestnut groves, and later flower-strewn old vineyards, pastures and the remains of a 'snail farm'! The lower western shoulder of the summit carries a communications mast, but this hasn't spoilt my enjoyment, it has increased it, as the resulting dirt road leading to the summit is a great improvement on the previous stony goat tracks. Don't let it spoil yours!

The Route

From the Panorama Taverna walk E and SE on the side of the road to the replacement bridge over the River Tiflos, pass E through the settlement of Katsomatados, leaving it beyond the small church of Saint Christos alongside the musical stream running through sweet chestnut and thriving olive groves. Gradually ascending E, ignore the right fork, and 150 paces beyond leave the eastbound

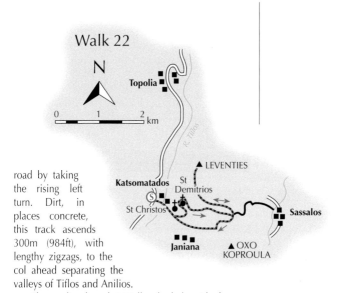

Walk 22

N

0   1   2 km

Topolia

R. Tiflos

▲ LEVENTIES

Katsomatados   St
                    Demitrios

St Christos

Sassalos

Janiana   ▲ OXO
              KOPROULA

road by taking
the rising left
turn. Dirt, in
places concrete,
this track ascends
300m (984ft), with
lengthy zigzags, to the
col ahead separating the
valleys of Tiflos and Anilios.

Flower lined and initially shaded, with fine
views into Topolia Gorge, pass the chapel of Saint
Demitrios, winding over the southern shoulders of
Leventies to arrive at the gated col above. Note S the
abandoned village of Janiana (1) over the valley below
Oxo Koproula. Rest at the crosstracks on the col and
admire the canvas of valley, ridge and mountain views.

Turn left, i.e. N (do not pass through the gate), to
ascend the dirt road, and at a large overhang on the left
the track turns right, giving us glimpses of half-hidden
Saint Athanasios (Walk 23), and to the north, the Gulf of
Kissamos bounded by Rodopou and Gramvousa peninsulas. Ahead turn left at the first fork, compass bearing
310°, ascending sharply towards the southern summit of
Leventies. Note a marker pillar to the left and also tiered,
flattened areas bounded with stones (2) that up to the
1950s were vineyards, pastures and snail-fattening sites.

Further ascent reveals the only minus of the walk, as
two communication masts appear alongside the bare,

exposed summit rocks of sharp-edged and pitted stone (pumice/volcanic lava). For those who wish to experience life at the top, leave the dirt track some 100m S of the two masts and their throbbing generators, to ascend right, picking one of many bare soil routes through jagged rocks for a not-too-difficult ascent to the solid, cairned grandstand summit.

Views of coastline, gorge, valley and mountain (3) enthral and excite, for from this seat in the 'gods' there are nineteen walks within this guide that can be identified. Descend with care to the track of ascent, following it down S and SE to the crosstracks on the gated col for an alternative return to Katsomatados.

Descend W, passing a solitary tree on the left, to the first double elbow. In the light and shade of early evening, valleys below present an atmospheric picture, accompanied by a chorus of goats, sheep, raptors, songbirds and humming bees. Turn sharp left for a winding descent via the old way to Katsomatados, overgrown in places with oleander and scrub, and scarred with small landslips. It is however a safe descent.

Before the chestnuts and olives, pass through a 'penned' section alongside an old *spiliari* (4) and two retired cars stuffed with animal feed and milk pails. At the streamside junction ahead turn right into the shade of sweet chestnuts, descending W through the gated groves to Katsomatados.

Leventies' summit

Items of Interest

(1) **JANIANA**. One of many deserted villages (see Baduriana, Walk 27) standing sightless and silent throughout Crete. For a short half-day/evening stroll from Katsomatatados, this silent place can be reached 1km (²/₃ mile) east and southeast from Katsomatados, through the olive groves. Many reasons account for the depopulation – Venetian (1204–1669) and Turkish (1669–1898) incursions and two world wars did little to stabilise the rural economy of indigenous Crete.

(2) **FARMING**. Goats, sheep and donkeys thrived on this high, rocky land, as did vines producing juicy grapes. Stranger still was the nurturing of snails, a great delicacy. Villagers collected the newly emerged snails in April, and fed and fattened them on breadcrumbs, which also removed the bitter flavour that came from their diet of grass.

(3) **VIEWS FROM LEVENTIES**. Leventies is Cretan Greek for 'Strong, Upstanding and Cretan'. North, the Topolia Gorge, below Topolia, spills into Tiflos Valley, leading the eye to the Gulf of Kissamos, Gramvousa and Rodopou. Over narrow Anilios Valley the walls of Halasses Gorge lead to Kandanos and the heights of Achinopodas. Due south lies Paleochora and the Libyan Sea. Closer to home, look southwest towards Kissamos' highest mountain, Agios Dikeos

(4) *SPILIARI*. Known also as *mitato* or *koumi* in other regions, *spilari* are invariably circular, drystone-wall structures, a shelter and store for shepherds and goatherds.

WALK 23

*By Gorge and Ridge to a
Monastery and Valley*

Katsomatados, Saint Athanassios, the Gorge,
Mouri, Latziana, Kapsaniana, Tiflos Valley, Topolia

Distance	13.6km (8½ miles)
Height Gain	350m (1148ft)
Start/Finish	Katsomatados/Topolia
Grade	3
Walking Time	6 hours
Maps	EFSTATHIADIS 1:79,000 CHANIA ISBN 960 226 531 0
	harms IC verlag 1:100,000 Western Crete (includes E4)
	ISBN 3–927468–16–9
Accommodation	Katsomatados, Topolia

A varied, challenging walk, with distant views and immediate surrounds, that constantly changes as olives give way to chestnut groves, open ridges and a narrow gorge. Underfoot, with the exception of stone- and scrub-filled Athanassios Gorge, paths and tracks present no navigational or restrictive problems. Villages, churches and ancient Vavara Monastery interest and delight, before the final ascent to Topolia.

The Route
Pass through Katsomatados, with its church, left, and proceed E, gradually ascending for 2km (1¼ miles), through chestnut and olive groves, alongside the tinkling stream. Leave the stream as the concrete track rises and swings left onto a dirt track, passing a dilapidated *spilari,* sheep pens and feeding troughs. Seven elbowed zigzags lead to the gated col above the scrub- and conifer-clad hillside. Pass through the gate (leave as found) and turn left, i.e. N, at this fine viewpoint.

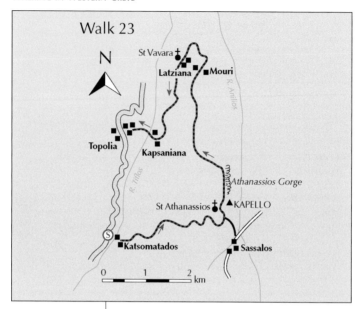

Continue along the scenic sloping track alongside vineyards for several hundred metres. At the first track junction left, turn left, to meet the tiny isolated and fenced church of Saint Athanassios at the head of Athanassios Gorge (1), overlooked to the right by the domed summit of Kapello ('hat'). Leave the church via a wire gate N onto a narrow path to a deep trench. Cross with care onto a narrow path N, passing a clutch of plane trees at the mouth of the gorge. The 0.75km (½ mile) descent over rocks and a thin dirt path, waymarked in places by splodges of red paint, is a bit of an adventure. You may have a wire-gated fence to negotiate halfway down, before emerging through a tight tangle of boulders and giant sage onto a wide, curving dirt track. A directional marker, 'Mouri', indicates left.

Mouri lies 2km (1¼ miles) N via the winding track that veers NW then N, through a profusion of olive groves and later vineyards and fruit trees. People are seldom seen along this dirt then concrete track, although it provides fine mountain views E to the summit rim of Halasses Gorge as Mouri comes into view.

This ancient and modern village, surrounded by vines and glistening lemons, provides a halfway house. Leave via the tarmac road N to a junction before the Church of Saint Nikolaos, with views of massive Rodopou visible ahead. Turn left here onto a dirt track, as indicated by an arrow 'ΛATZIANA – 1250m' (English except the first letter Λ – a Greek L). Ascend towards a white building then veer right, making for a tower as the track rises between olives and vines.

At the next T-junction, with a sign telling us 'We have come from Mouri – 700m', turn left over a spur onto a flower-lined track descending S to Latziana. Marvel at the dramatic jaws of Topolia Gorge below and ahead, and to the right the summits of Profitas Ilias above Platanos. The few houses of Latziana are met, half hidden in a profusion of stately platania, acer and castanea.

The highlight of this small settlement, apart from the friendliness of its inhabitants, is the crumbling remains of its ancient monastery, dedicated to Saint Vavara (Saint Barbara) (2). Access is gained from the angle of the junction of road and track by a giant plane tree. Walk down to the entrance of Saint Vavara, following the arrowhead directing left on a thin grass path to the now visible monastery. Take care underfoot and alongside the crumbling monastery walls and arches when examining the ruins.

Leave Latziana SSW at its junction, descending to Kapsaniana via a series of zigzags and U-bends. Many tracks/footpaths join/leave the main descending track – ignore them and use the conspicuous northern jaws of Topolia Gorge to the south as your overall marker. Underfoot the tarmac gives way to a farm twintrack as we begin the journey to Kapsaniana – indicated by a yellow arrowhead 'Maptziana' (Kapsaniana) between two giant platania and some water taps dated 1959. Ten minutes from Latziana we meet another T-junction and the remains of several old village houses. Carry straight on, making for the northern mouth of Topolia Gorge, passing a pristine white chapel on the right. Ignore side tracks unless they head for the gorge, and continue descending to meet another T-junction. Here you turn right, i.e. N, on a more level track (above on the ridgeway note the conspicuous mast seen above Mouri) to zigzag, descending to Kapsaniana – a walk of 20 minutes from Latziana. You may be greeted at the first house by a barrage of barking dogs, fortunately tethered, as the road winds down to the concrete bridge over the River Tiflos. To the right is the olive-press factory (3).

Once over this functional bridge turn immediately left onto a dirt pathway rising steeply to Topolia. Ascend initially S, then E of S (watch out for dozing snakes (4)), via a series of U-bends that provide an insight into the northern end of Topolia Gorge, passing clumps of bamboo before a concrete track rising right to the flower-lined cemetery and principal church of Saint Evangelistra. Topolia is pleasing and friendly, but time your arrival to avoid the afternoon siesta.

Athanassios Gorge north

138

Items of Interest

(1) **ATHANASSIOS GORGE**. A deep, narrow cleft descending south to north that allows passage into the fertile plateau of the Mouri Ridge. Water beneath the pitted volcanic boulders, similar to those crowning the summit of nearby Leventies (Walk 22), is plentiful judging by the abundance of vegetation, particularly sage, which grows in 'bush' form. This cleft restricts direct sunlight into the floor of the gorge, a phenomenon much appreciated by resident goats.

(2) **SAINT VAVARA**. An eleventh-century Byzantine monastery of some importance, now sadly in ruins and overrun with goats.

(3) **OLIVE OIL FACTORIES**. Kissamos is fertile and well able to nourish 'the golden tree' – the olive tree – that covers three-quarters of Crete's fertile land, providing the entire population with a nutritious diet, cooking oil, fuel, light, heat, and wood for building material. Olives are harvested in autumn and early winter and taken to the oil factory for pressing. The first two cold pressings produce virgin olive oil and premium oil. Subsequent hot water pressings provide oil for soap manufacture, and the solid remains are mixed into animal feed or used as fertiliser. Little wonder the Cretans live so long.

(4) **SLEEPING SNAKES**. A word of warning – on the ascent to Topolia, Greta was just about to step over what she thought was a broken branch when 'it' suddenly spiralled into the undergrowth as she simultaneously gyrated skywards to land approximately 4 metres away from the fast-disappearing metre-long snake. Amusing after the event, maybe, but do take care and watch where you place your feet.

WALK 24

A Scenic Sunday Walk

*Vlatos, Milia Road, Trapeza,
Tsourouniana, Topolia*

Distance	8.8km (5½ miles)
Height Gain	200m (656ft)
Start/Finish	Vlatos/Topolia
Grade	2–3
Walking Time	3 hours
Maps	EFSTATHIADIS 1:79,000 CHANIA ISBN 960 226 531 0
	harms IC verlag 1:100,000 Western Crete (includes E4)
	ISBN 3–927468–16–9
Accommodation	Topolia, plus refreshments; taxi if required

An elevated, linear journey north contours the western slopes of picturesque Tiflos Valley on quiet country lanes, dirt and stone tracks and an
old, slabbed donkey track. Airy and scenic, the journey supplies constant,
varied views. The abundant and colourful wildlife provides pleasing companions, particularly the birds.

The Route

There are two outstanding landmarks in the drawn-out
village of Vlatos. At the east end stands an ancient,
imposing platania (plane tree) (1) alongside a fine taverna
of the same name. At the west end is the striking church
of Saint Maria (Panagia). It matters not which one you
choose to start from, although if you start from the
Platania Taverna you see them both, plus the friendly,
well-tended village. Leave Vlatos, beyond the pristine
walls of the church, at the T-junction by the
Environmental Centre. Turn right – signposted 'Milia' –
to pass by the remaining houses, noisy dogs and a closed

school. Flourishing olive groves and impressive trees line the route as the ascending road spirals N to meet another signposted junction. Turn right with the Milia road, passing a small vineyard, on a tree-lined, undulating road to an acute elbow with shaded seats and water fountain, the gateway to the arboretum known as the 'Park of Peace' (2).

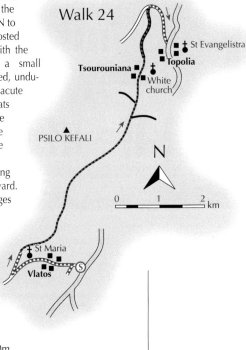

Leave the pleasing trees, ascending eastward. The tarmac soon changes to dirt and stone as it adopts a winding N, NE course for the next 4.5km (2¾ miles) above the Tiflos Valley. This is a stimulating journey, between the 450m (1476ft) and 550m (1805ft) contours, and below the scrub- and conifer-clad summit ridge of Psilo Kefali, 901m (2956ft) to the west. Birds of many species please the eyes and ears, and in spring colourful flowers lighten the step. Distant views E beyond Tiflos Valley also tempt, as do the immediate views into the southern jaws of Topolia Gorge and the bare summit rock of Leventies (Walk 22), its eastern bastion.

At the signposted junction, with its path descending right to Katsomatados, continue N with the 'Milia' finger-post for approximately 50m to a fork branching right, where the Milia track veers left. Ascend N and NNE via

Saint Maria (Panagia), Vlatos

the recent tarmac road that zigzags through rock- and scrub-clad summits. Solitude surrounds this carpet of colour, known as 'Trapeza', high above Topolia Gorge and the cave of Saint Sophia (Walk 18). Birdsong fills the air and birds of prey soar overhead with ease as the elevated route sweeps between the surrounding mini summits to eventually descend right, i.e. E, with a series of sharp U-bends.

With the acute zigzag behind, our tarmac lane eventually meets an incoming dirt track on the right. Ignore the incomer and continue descending slightly, approximately N, with the tree-lined lane, soon to meet an ancient, stone-laid twintrack on the right. Take this original stone-stepped donkey track, right, descending through olive groves, fruit trees and vegetable gardens to the scattered, pleasant village of Tsourouniana. Underfoot this old track, prone to double as a stream after heavy rain, reaches a U-bend in the road at the village perimeter. Take the right-hand road N to the pristine white village church, the departure point should you wish to explore this pleasant place with its musical stream.

From the church surrounds, walk N on tarmac ascending for 1.6km (1 mile) for a pleasing, tree-lined hike to the col above Topolia. Just before the col the road joins the Kalathenes–Topolia road (this relatively new road is not shown on listed maps). Here you may meet the occasional vehicle en route to Topolia, an inconvenience that is compensated for by extensive views of sea, peninsula, mountain, valley and Topolia Gorge that greet us from the col (3). Descend S, passing the great oak of Topolia, reputed to be the 'Methuselah' of Cretan oaks, spanning the road. Beyond stands Topolia Gorge and the hillside village of Topolia.

Items of Interest

(1) **PLATANIA**. *Platanus orientalis*, the plane tree, is perhaps the most efficient 'water-diviner' in Crete. These trees grow to a great size, as seen in the oldest (claims vary from 1400 to 1500 years) and largest platania in Crete, gracing Vlatos. Together with sweet chestnut it attracts the parasitic ivy (*Herbera helix*) whose wood is much sought-after by craftsmen producing the resonant Cretan lyre.

(2) **PARK OF PEACE**. Planted in 1976 by the Bavarian authorities as a gesture of reconciliation for the denudation of timber, 1941–45, by Nazi Germans. Bavarian forest rangers return annually to tend this cool and quiet place of woodland walks.

(3) **VIEWS**. North into the fertile Tiflos Valley, a sea of olive green scattered with white villages, and beyond the Gulf of Kissamos' blue waters flanked by the imposing peninsulas of Gramvousa left, and Rodopou right. East beyond the Tiflos and Anilios valleys ridges lead the eye to the encircling ranges surrounding Kandanos.

WALK 25

Agios Dikeos, the Olympus of Kissamos

*Elos, Infant River Tiflos, Sweet
Chestnuts, Information Board, Summit
Chapel of Saint Dikeos, Elos*

Distance	6km (3¾ miles)
Height Gain	685m (2247ft)
Start/Finish	Elos/Elos
Grade	3 to 4 depending on weather
Walking Time	Ascent 3 hours, descent 2½ hours
Maps	'Wanderkarte' KRETA Chania, 1:79,000
	harms IC verlag 1:100,000 Western Crete
	ISBN 3–927468–16–9
Accommodation	Rooms and refreshment in Elos

The ascent of Dikeos, at 1184m (3885ft) the highest point in Kissamos, is, contrary to local conception, a pleasant and rewarding mountain hike via a series of ascending dirt and stone zigzag roads and tracks. No rock scrambles, arêtes, swaying suspension bridges over gullies, glaciers or sections of high exposure impede passage. The narrow roads/tracks to the summit are courtesy of NATO, built to service the radar devices on Dikeos and the three observation 'golf balls' capping adjoining Tsounara to the southwest. Scenically it's one of the best grandstands in Western Crete. Watch out on the summit for vultures hanging on the thermals, waiting for exhausted walkers! Dikeos is not difficult, it's just high!

The Route

From the main street bus stop, in the centre of straggling Elos, walk S from the east end of Taverna Filoxenia. Ascend the zigzag road passing impressive domed St John's Church. At the cemetery junction take the right-hand route swinging left past a chickenhouse, before leaving the chestnut-lined road right, crossing a ford adjacent to a malodorous pigsty by a scatter of giant rocks lining the eroded, descending watercourse. Swing left, rounding the pigsty, ascending the wide dirt track S alongside the rock-strewn water into the chestnut grove (1).

As you ascend, veer left to cross the riverbed, via a sagging ford, to begin the serious, but not difficult, ascent of Dikeos' endless zigzags that rise 500m (1640ft) to the summit. Once over the ford note the University of Iraklion's information panel regarding the protection of the bearded vulture (2). The chestnut-shaded way thins out as we pound the dirt and stone tracks, giving way to scrub and, in spring, colourful flowers. This is home to singing birds, sheep and goats, and as height is gained only goats (3). Now 700m (2297ft) above sea level, with the chestnut trees below and the summit visible above, cross the last of the feeder streams of the infant River Tiflos. Scrub predominates amid the protruding rock, and as it will be several hours before shade is available (apart from an indoor summit sojourn), **protect your head**.

Views into the Tiflos plateau floor and slopes below, from the skirts of Dikeos to Topolia Gorge and surrounding mountains, are awash with the greens of olive and chestnut interspersed by scattered white villages. The mountain's vegetation is dominated by prickly perennials and endemic cyclamen (*Cyclamen creticum*).

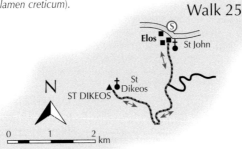

Walk 25

145

Summit chapel of Saint Dikeos

Climbing again, via the snaking sweeps of the dirt and stone road, the upper Tiflos Valley (plateau) to the north opens up. The final ascent, with ever-shortening zigzags, provides eagle's-eye views of the three N–S-running ridges of Dikeos, and all of Kissamos and Selinos.

Finally the summit is revealed from my favourite bend – not the last one, but one that displays the grey-walled chapel of Saint Dikeos plus the large, incongruous radar detectors, and on three peaks SW, the 'golf balls' of NATO on Tsounara. Somehow the final metres become a leisurely stroll as the humming towers are passed and we enter through the 'cross-capped' metal gate into the protective 1883 Chapel and Bothy of Agios Dikeos, with its 1993 supply of fresh water. The views are as eye-catching as they are extensive (4).

Descent is via the route of ascent, and with the mountain now behind us a panorama unfolds N and E. Don't hurry; make the descending leg a leisurely stroll.

Items of Interest

(1) **ELOS**. Elos is the principal village of Inahorion ('Nine Villages') and site of ancient Kufi Kara – Archontica. All

nine nestle on the high, fertile plateau ringed by Dikeos, Plakoselia, Koutrouli, Kolibos, Psilo Kefali, Leventies, Oxo Koproula and Metarizia. A land of milk and honey, with Elos at the hub of Crete's sweet-chestnut production, with more trees than people, it also produces the strawberry tree (Arbutus unedo), from whose berries raki, the local spirit, is distilled.

(2) **THE BEARDED VULTURE**. Together with other vultures, eagles, buzzards and falcons within Crete, they are protected species under Greek law. The habitat of these raptors is mountainous, e.g. Dikeos, and includes the Tiflos river and valley to the Topolia Gorge.

(3) **MOUNTAIN SHEEP AND GOATS**. Sheep are quiet, unobtrusive animals that walk the mountain slopes in single file, with heads held low. Goats in contrast are more excitable, bell-ringing, wind-breaking beasts that prefer the higher ground and coarser vegetation. They are in my opinion more intelligent than sheep, as they appear to understand the guttural, very loud, local 'goat speak' commands, such as '*Hah*', '*Naah*', '*Uhh*' and '*Ugh*', roared out by goatherds when directing their herds to fresh grazing or for milking, and also to left or right.

(4) **SUMMIT VIEWS**. **East** – to and over Kandanos and the heights of Achinopodas, rear the dramatic summits of Psilafi, Gingilos and Volaki, hiding the great gorge of Samaria, but not the snow-capped peaks of the Lefka Ori (White Mountains). **South** – over rippling ridges to Paleochora and Akrotiri Krios and beyond to the Libyan Sea. **Southwest** – over the mountain village of Sklavopoula lies the azure lagoon of Elafonisos and the 'golden stepped' Monastery of Chrisoskalitissis. **West** – over Stomio Gorge to the rocky coastline north to Sfinari Bay. **North** – over the Tiflos plateau to sugarloaf Profitas Ilias, ancient Polyrinia, Kastelli, and the Gulf of Kissamos framed by its twin peninsulas.

WALK 26

Inahorion – So Many Shades of Green

Elos, Limni, Rogdia, Vlatos

Distance	7.6km (4¾ miles)
Height Gain	137m (450ft)
Start/Finish	Elos/Vlatos
Grade	2
Walking Time	3 hours
Maps	'Wanderkarte' KRETA Chania, 1:79,000
	harms IC verlag 1:100,000 Western Crete
	ISBN 3–927468–16–9
Accommodation	Rooms in Elos, refreshment in all four villages

A stroll through the foothills of upper Tiflos Valley utilising quiet country lanes and tracks through vineyards, olive groves and stands of chestnut, oak, pine and plane. Rich in indigenous flora and fauna, with panoramic views of Tiflos Valley and its surrounds and enhanced by four charming villages. One village, Rogdia, is divided by height into three, another, Vlatos, lays claim to the oldest and largest plane tree in Crete.

The Route

The delightful hill-foot village of Limni ('lake') is 0.75km (½ mile) N from the east end of Lower Elos via a rising country lane. An alternative route, from Upper Elos, rises N and W to the col above Elos; although taking longer to Limni, 2km (1¼ miles), it provides a fine grandstand from which to view the massif of Dikeos and Tiflos Valley.

Beyond the roadside *cantina*, approaching Elos, a series of highway zigzags lead to the village. One zigzag bend, opposite a large house, is extremely acute and marks the point at which we leave the road for a tarmac

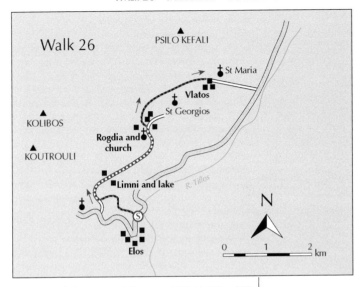

and dirt track that proceeds in an arc NW–N–NE and W through a depression containing olives and the occasional chestnut grove. Pass two farmhouses on the looping track through the basin to emerge, via a short steep track, onto the country lane leading N and NE from the col above Elos to Limni.

Above, to the north, tower the rocky peaks of Koutrouli 1068m (3504ft) and Kolibos 1033m (3398ft); to the south note the giant umbrella-like trees fronting the scatter of white buildings of Elos, before reaching the elongated village of Limni (1). Lake and village are heralded by a stately oak on the right and a new taverna, very close to the tree-clad banks of The Lake, before the village name sign. First impressions are of a relatively modern village, the majority of dwellings flanking the elongated main street, but not so if you look at the giant, gnarled village olive trees and the crumbling olive oil press on the slopes above.

Ascending slightly, leave the village with the roadway curving NE, and as the last house is left behind pause awhile on the small mound right of the road to admire the extensive views.

Geometrically patterned olive groves, pastures and vineyards, singing and soaring birds, endless rising ridges and rocky mountain tops greet the walker. Views constantly change as this highroad winds NE and N to the lower of the three half-hidden Rogdia settlements below the rock of Kolibos, an entrance marked by a graveyard of dead and dying plane trees, victims of parasites who devour the fruit, leaves, etc. There are also several ancient, gnarled olive trees of extraordinary girth, indicating how long Rogdia has existed.

The three settlements of Kato (lower), Meso (middle), and Apano (upper) Rogdia, clinging to a steep spur that rises to the summit ridge of Kolibos, are in the form of an inverted cone 100–150m (328–492ft) high. The ascent from Kato to Apano is courtesy of a steep, flower-lined series of sharp, tarmac zigzags, that rise left, i.e. N, immediately past the towered church. Ascent is rapid as layer upon layer of tidy houses and noisy dogs are passed, to reach and pass what many imagine is the final and highest house. The track, above a large concrete water tank, rises higher on the left; opposite note the yellow, blue-rimmed Milia waymarks. Above and left, hidden among the summit trees, are the final few houses of Apano Rogdia (only two appeared to be occupied at the time of writing).

Ignore the track left to these old houses and take the waymarked way above the water tank to contour the spur E on a narrow tarmac road. A small chapel hoves into view at a fork in the road. Take the dirt track right to pass the chapel, descending by olive groves and venerable chestnuts. Birds of prey spiral effortlessly above the track, which rises left at yet another fork, where olives line the approach to the well-maintained Church of Saint Georgios. Shaded benches and a table surround the small church, providing extensive views particularly into the NE/SE quadrant over Vlatos, half hidden in the olive-green groves of the valley.

Continue N and NE from Saint Georgios, descending on a twisting dirt track – steep sections coated in concrete – passing the occasional house of the old settlement of Bertigiana. Beyond, link with the Vlatos–Milia road above the prominent, now visible church of Saint Maria (Panagia) at the west end of Vlatos. This waymarked junction directs right to a second junction, by the Environmental Centre, where it is left for Kato Vlatos beyond Saint Maria (2), then E into the delightful, somewhat drawn-out, olive- and fruit-tree-surrounded, rose-bedecked village. No accommodation, but alongside Vlatos' ancient platania (3) stands Taverna Platania, one of Crete's finest, signposted and situated 100m (50m on the sign) into the olive groves at the east end of the village. There can be no finer finish to any walk than at the Taverna of Costis and family by the giant plane tree in Vlatos.

Items of Interest

(1) **LIMNI**. The small lake at the west end of the village, a rare feature in Crete, is the first of two in the Prefecture of Chania, the other being the larger Lake Kournas, east of Chania. Size wise, Limni could be classified as a pond, but visually it deserves its name, its dark waters surrounded by water-hungry chestnut trees. Frogs, if the volume of their croaking is an indicator, love Limni.

(2) **SAINT MARIA (*PANAGIA*)**. A pristine holy place, with domed red pantiles and fresh, pale-yellow walls, its main door is flanked by marble with black inscriptions. Two dates, 1958 and 8–9–1968, may suggest renovation or rebuilding, for the external twin bells, by the side of the church (in bas relief the 'Virgin Mary and Baby Jesus'), carry the date 1872. Also above the main church door, in goldleaf, is a mythical two-headed eagle with wings outstretched, holding in its clawed feet what appear to be two globes of the Earth. On and between its twin heads sits a golden crown topped centrally by a simple cross.

'The largest and oldest plane tree', at Vlatos

(3) **PLANE TREE**. A massive, venerable specimen with several trunks and a spread of 50m, its hollowed-out main trunk, by the local stream and taverna of the same name, has cradled many a sleeping local boy. The tree is reputed to have seen 1400 summers!

WALK 27

*A Crater, a Donkey Track
and a Seat in the 'Gods'*

*Elos, Louhia/Lohia, the great hole/crater,
Baduriane, Limni, Elos*

Distance	8.25km (4¼ miles)
Height Gain	250m (820ft)
Start/Finish	Elos/Elos
Grade	3
Walking Time	4 hours
Maps	'Wanderkarte' KRETA Chania, 1:79,000
	Harms IC verlag 1:100,000 Western Crete
	ISBN 3–927468–16–9
Accommodation	Rooms in Elos; refreshment at Elos and Limni

A ridge walk providing a peep into the mysterious crater on the Elos/Louhia Col, and a framed, eagle's-eye view into picturesque Tiflos Valley, cradled by mountain ridges and backed to the east-southeast by the distant peaks above Kandanos. Dirt and stone tracks lead to and from a high-level donkey track, with carpets of flowers, flanked in places by olive groves, vineyards, chestnuts and platania. Overhead, vultures and screeching eagles swoop and soar in search of food. This easy-to-navigate scenic delight also passes through Limni, with its lake.

The Route

Beyond the roadside *cantina*, on the northeastern flanks of Elos, a series of zigzags leads to the town centre. Before the centre, by a sharp-angled bend opposite a prominent house, leave the road on a tarmac and dirt track curving NW–N–NE and W through olive and chestnut groves. Two farmhouses are passed, as the

153

northern flanks and summit of Dikeos above Elos can be seen, as well as the Limni road, above to the north. Ascend, via a short steep track, onto the quiet road to turn left, i.e. S, leading to the signposted triple junction on the Elos/Louhia Col.

From this fine grandstand descend SW/NW with the twisting tarmacked main road into the head of the Stomio Valley via a series of bends that reveal ahead and above Louhia's distinctive church and burial ground to the right. Leave the road right onto a concrete track ascending to the church (1), dated 1885, its tight-packed cemetery and tree-hidden, declining village. Leave by walking E on a thin path alongside the north wall of the white church, rising with a fence on the right for a few metres, before a U-bend in a grass-centred dirt and stone track. With this track ascend N, passing vineyards and olive groves, note the extensive views W over and beyond Perivolia (Walk 29).

The fenced track swings left, rising over a shoulder ridge from the heights of Koutrouli, 1068m (3504ft), ahead. Interesting though the Munro might be, it is a huge crater (2), visible below right, as the track swings NE, i.e. left, which fascinates. **Do not** attempt further inspection from this point. Beyond, descend NE and N over the ridge shoulder onto a concrete track leading left to a wide dirt and stone road, ascending N and E via a series of zigzags. The route is via this road, rounding seven U-bends until the U-bend that bears two arrowhead Milia waymarks ▶ is reached, one directing W to Milia, the other from Milia. At this point leave the wide dirt/stone road to join (with care over a water-washed stony ditch) seven stone steps 20m N that lead to a wire gate opening onto a fine donkey track.

Old donkey tracks are my favourites when traversing the high ground of Crete, and this one ranks with the best, not only underfoot, but also for views E and S (3). In places, however, this descending track across the middle slopes of Koutrouli may appear, to those who have not experienced these high-level walkways, as exposed and precarious. They need not fear, **providing they place their feet with care and stop to admire the views**.

Soon the contouring, and later descending, scrub-lined donkey track peters out to arrive at the stony remains of the traditional hill village of Baduriana, its houses animal shelters now, silent sentinels of centuries past. Pick your way carefully over stone and rock on a visible, tiered path between the old houses to open onto a wider track, which by a series of sweeping U-bends leads S and E, descending quite steeply towards a T-junction by conifer, castanea and olives, passing the old olive press of Limni.

The Church of Evangelismos of Theotokos, Louhia

Emerging from the shady, chestnut-lined track onto the main street of Limni, turn right, i.e. W, past the roadside lake with its goldfish and frogs, to our initial point of emergence, before the Elos/Louhia Col. When the steep track is met, turn left onto the outward route from Elos for a pleasant, arborial return to Elos.

Items of Interest
(1) **LOUHIA CHURCH**. The bell of Evangelismos of Theotokos is devoid of name and manufacturer, but the interior of the church is graced by a fine, glass-and-brass chandelier, and its graveyard is full of elegant, flower-decorated marble tombstones. This stately, peaceful place provides wonderful views west-southwest into bountiful Stomio Valley.

(2) **LOUHIA CRATER**. This great basin, of formidable proportions, has a flat floor on which only grasses grow, with a small area retaining a shallow pond. Its steep sides are tree and scrub clad. It is not a manmade quarry, but more likely the result of a landslip similar to the smaller one in neighbouring Limni that created The Lake (Walk 25). Local opinion emphatically states that this crater has, in Scots vernacular, 'aye been'.

(3) **DONKEY TRACK VIEWS**. South-southeast, over a surging sea of varying greens to the hill-foot township of Elos, the principal town and sweet-chestnut capital of the Municipality of Inahorion (Nine Villages). Above the scattered white houses to the south rise wrinkled ridges, cradles of the infant River Tiflos, which begins its lengthy journey north to the blue waters of the Gulf of Kissamos. Higher still is the summit of Dikeos, crowned by the walled white church of Saint Dikeos, and higher still by a family of soaring eagles and vultures.

WALK 28

The Lonely Valley to Sassalos

Junction Strovles/Aligi, Platilakos Valley, Sassalos

Distance	9km (6 miles)
Height Gain	150m (492ft)
Start/Finish	T-Junction between Strovles and Aligi/ Sassalos
Grade	3
Walking Time	4 hours
Maps	EFSTATHIADIS 1:79,000 CHANIA ISBN 960 226 531 0
	harms IC verlag 1:100,000 Western Crete (includes E4)
	ISBN 3–927468–16–9
Accommodation: Katsomatados	

A descending journey that will test your navigational skills but not your stamina. It is initially north, on a winding way through rounded hills, taking undulating tracks and pathways that provide ever-changing scenery as each corner is turned. Paths however vary, particularly in the second half, when the valley floor narrows and surrounding scrub and woodland envelop the paths, changing their make up and visible presence. Here experience and compass are helpful. Fortunately we have a guide – a tiny, in summer dry, occasionally waymarked stream. Close ups of the varied indigenous wildlife grace this lonely, but friendly, valley. Sassalos, a scattered, pleasant village (with limited refreshments available in 2004) arrives all too soon.

The Route

Start from the multiple junction 1km (²/₃ mile) SSE from Strovles and 1.25km (¾ mile) NW from Aligi, reached either by taxi, Kastelli-to-Paleochora school bus, or a lift by car. Take the concrete paved track ascending E, marked by a blank signboard, 30m E from the road signs

'Paleochora 25km' SE/S and 'Voutas' SW. Agios Dikeos' omnipresent bulk dominates the western skyline. At the 500m (1640ft) contour, ascend E and later N on the intermittent concrete then dirt track, zigzagging to the 650m (2133ft) contour after approximately 1km (⅔ mile).

Ascend beyond the beehives (1) to the col ahead on a scrub- and shrub-lined way, prominent amongst which are *koomaros* (2). The concrete underfoot ends yet again at a crossroads, where a blue arrowhead on a roadside stone directs right on the rising track, NE and N, to the col. At the next meeting of tracks take the right-hand way, E then N and NE, before a wiremesh gate.

Aligi is now visible to the SE, with extensive views to the eastern boundaries of Kissamos and Selinos, flanked by rounded hills and olive-green ridges. Below right are valleys of silver-green olives, sectioned by a network of roads and tracks liberally sprinkled with red-tiled, white-walled churches.

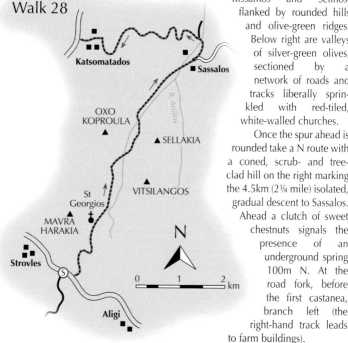

Once the spur ahead is rounded take a N route with a coned, scrub- and tree-clad hill on the right marking the 4.5km (2¾ mile) isolated, gradual descent to Sassalos. Ahead a clutch of sweet chestnuts signals the presence of an underground spring 100m N. At the road fork, before the first castanea, branch left (the right-hand track leads to farm buildings).

Sassalos

Continue the gradual descent N, overlooked by steep-sided, tree- and scrub-clad ridges with conical summits. Side valleys spill down, vultures and eagles circle above, and continuous birdsong fills the air. Our guide is the wide dirt track, descending between N and NNE, eventually arriving at a clearing with a lively stream (3) running through. Cross the waters by ford to the half-hidden small church (4) (undergoing restoration 2003–4), beneath a massive plane tree.

Leave the church, with your back to its southern side, by turning left onto a twintrack, which later becomes a single pathway after entering a tree, bush and scrub tunnel. This takes us on a red-paint-dotted marked route, bearing 20° E of N (plus or minus 5°), below overhanging trees, through bracken and dwarf conifer. Cross the stream at waymarked points on somewhat unstable stepping stones. Eventually, by compass work alongside or over the stream, emerge through a wiremesh fence onto a wet riverside track and pasture that transforms into a wide dirt track bound for Sassalos.

Ascending N on the west side of the river take the lower left fork, i.e. 20° E of N, as houses appear through the omnipresent olives. Ahead, past the cemetery, the concrete way leads to the red-domed, pantiled Sassalos Church of Saint Irini. Beyond, cross the Anilios river to a tarmac road bearing signs to 'Floria' and 'Milones'. Turn left, i.e. N, to the village store and *cafenion* for refreshments (limited). In 2004 the store closed, but new owners hopefully will be found.

Alternative Ending

An alternative to ending the walk in Sassalos is to extend it to Katsomatados by foot, where food and beds are available. This is a walk of 4km (2½ miles) with an ascent of 200m (656ft) to the 500m (1640ft) high col W, and a descent of 300m (984ft).

Leave Sassalos, via the descending roadway behind the village store, to cross the Anilios river W by ford. At the Y-junction ahead, below several houses, flanked by a pencil-thin cypress tree, take the left fork W to an initially descending dirt track which fluctuates, concrete to dirt to concrete, as it zigzags to the gated col above, leading to Katsomatados. Ascent provides sightings into the mouth of the dramatic Halasses Gorge.

At the col pause awhile to soak up the views near and far before descending W, past a lone tree on the left, to the first double elbow. Turn sharp left for the original winding descent to the olive and castanea groves of Katsomatados.

Items of Interest

(1) **BEES AND HONEY**. Where there are bees there are certain plants on which they feed and thrive; the converse also applies. Plants, in particular heather and thyme, not only sustain these tireless insects, but also give the resultant honey – *miele* or *méli* – its distinct and appealing Cretan flavour. Seasonal 'swarms' of blue and white hives and their busy, buzzing occupants provide local honey known as *thimo* or *thimomalos*. To receive a jar is an honour.

(2) *KOOMAROS*. This shrub-like Cretan tree thrives in Kissamos. Its early flowers appeal to bees, resulting in a

good, but somewhat bitter, honey. *Raki*, Western Crete's special spirit, is distilled from its cherry-like fruits in the latter part of the year.

(3) **FEEDER STREAM**. This stream, rushing from the flanks of Mayra Harakia, is a principal feeder of the River Anilios, waters that in times of flood thunder through the confines of the Halasses Gorge, preventing passage by foot.

(4) **SAINT GEORGIOS**. The church bell, when last I visited, was suspended from a nearby olive tree. Icons and murals inside the church are naturally dedicated to Saint George, whose name day is 2 June.

St Georgios' church

WALK 29

Into the Stomio Valley to Vathi

Louhia, Perivolia, Vathi

Distance	3.6km (2¼ miles) – double if return
Height Gain	Nil, 100m (328ft) if return
Start/Finish	Louhia Col/Vathi
Grade	1
Walking Time	1¼ hours, 2½ hours if return
Maps	'Wanderkarte' KRETA Chania, 1:79,000
	harms IC verlag 1:100,000 Western Crete
	ISBN 3–927468–16–9
Accommodation	Perivolia – rooms and refreshments; refreshments at Vathi

A gently descending walk, tree and flower lined, that includes two interesting, well-maintained, friendly villages, as well as an abundance of colourful wildlife. Wide pathways and tracks are utilised alongside the lively, rock-strewn watercourse, while above the gorge is ringed with scrub-clad mountains, some exceeding 1000m (3281ft).

The Route

From the col, W and above Elos, at the road junction from Limni, descend SW with the spiralling road to meet a concrete track descending left. If you wish to visit Louhia church – Evangelismos of Theotokos – visible ahead, right, and the village, it's a short return walk to the westerly bound concrete track. Descend on the concrete to a dirt track through the gorge, dropping and twisting through olive groves on a bearing of 240° magnetic. Alongside the tumbling stream sweet chestnut and gnarled olive trees provide shade. Ignore any side roads, and enjoy the constant birdsong, sweet-smelling honeysuckle, buzzing of bees, and even the croaking of vociferous frogs on the 1.5km (1 mile) to the tidy, interesting hamlet of Perivolia (1).

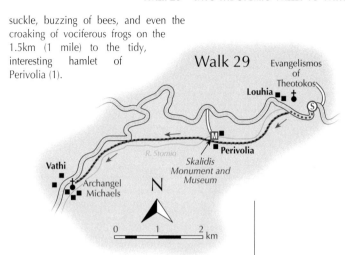

White and pastel-shaded walls and red-tiled roofs present a relaxed, sunlit village of proud, polite people. One small, ageing *cafenion*/taverna on the immediate left – it looks like a private house with tables and chairs – will serve a 2-inch-thick potato *omaletta* that has few equals and no superiors. The other larger taverna is modern by comparison, clean and friendly. Houses rise on the surrounding slopes as we drop down to cross the noisy waters of the Stomio/Perivolia River on a relatively new, concrete and tarmac bridge, or on the old bridge with its single arch minus its parapet. Note, as you pass by, the striking Skalidis Monument and Skalidis Museum.

Leave the village beyond the museum walking S, first on tarmac then concrete which reverts to dirt and stone, via a shady way with the ever-widening river on the left. The undulating track rises and falls as it descends overall for 1km (²/₃ mile), through continuous olive groves, to meet the circuitous main road, from Kefali far above, leading left into Vathi (2). As tidy, colourful and friendly as Perivolia, Vathi today spans the river and is expanding

Skalidis Monument at Perivolia

ΑΝΑΓΝΩΣΤΗΣ Γ. ΣΚΑΛΙΔΗΣ
ΓΕΝΙΚΟΣ ΑΡΧΗΓΟΣ ΚΙΣΑΜΟΥ
ΠΡΟΕΔΡΟΣ ΚΡΗΤΙΚΗΣ ΒΟΥΛΗΣ
1818 - 1901

to the south – our route for a future walk (Walk 31), which can, for those with the urge to explore much further, be an extension to this pleasing but short stroll. If not, explore Vathi, including the old ruined oil mill by the ford below the square, and enjoy the views and refreshments, or perhaps a haircut at the *cafenion/ouzeri* of Tassos, one of nature's gentlemen, overlooking the square.

Should you not wish to return to the col above Elos on foot, and if you prefer to save the Vathi–Tzitzifa–Plokamiana experience for another day, an afternoon bus, bound for Elos and Kastelli, passes through Vathi around 4.15pm. (Do check bus times.)

Items of Interest

(1) **PERIVOLIA**. Perivolia has an ancient 'port' or gateway and Greco-Roman tombs – thought to be first century BC. Also of interest, and much nearer the present day, is the Museum and Monument of Skalidis, renowned leader of the revolution against the occupying Turks. As recently as the 1941–45 conflict, Perivolia and many other townships and villages within Kissamos were again actively involved in ridding their country of another invader.

(2) **VATHI**. Vathi (old name Kuneni) has a fine church devoted to Archangel Michaels, and a square framed with flowers and the blue-and-white-striped flag of Greece, commemorating the local freedom fighters executed between 1941–45. It is the administrative centre of this district of hillside-clinging villages, seen only by the majority of visitors through vehicle windows, as they pass by on their way to the lagoon of Elafonisos.

WALK 30

To Saint Paraskevi on its Lofty Perch

Kefali, Saint Paraskevi, Papadiana, Kefali

Distance	9km (5½ miles)
Height Gain	250m (820ft)
Start/Finish	Kefali/Kefali
Grade	3
Walking Time	4½–5 hours
Maps	'Wanderkarte' KRETA Chania, 1:79,000
	harms IC verlag 1:100,000 Western Crete
	ISBN 3–927468–16–9
Accommodation	Rooms and refreshment in Kefali

A high-level walk above the green and fertile valley of Vathi and Stomio revealing 360° of surrounding mountains, gorges and valley floor, in company with soaring, swooping eagles and vultures, and in season a profusion of wild flowers. Ascents are never too demanding on the zigzag tracks to the in-need-of-restoration Church of Saint Paraskevi.

The Route

Leave Kefali's taverna-lined road, overlooking Stomio Valley, walking due W, passing on the right the statue of Nikolaos Pimplis (1) beside a shaded children's play area, and on the left one of my favourite tavernas, Jenny's 'ΕΛΑΦΟΣ', as the road swings left. Continue on this Papadiana-bound road for a short distance to swing right, rising steeply W between olive trees, to a road fork, Papadiana left, right the guest house waymarked 'Velenos'. Veer right and ascend to meet several large, aged houses ahead. Pass them, right, and ascend N via a concrete track, steep in places, zigzagging NE to NW, i.e. overall N.

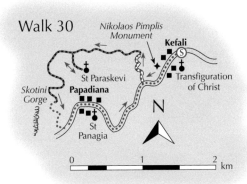

We now climb via a dirt track, zigzagging occasionally to the N. On our left a sizeable valley provides wide and interesting views as we pass four to five houses displaying traditional Inahorion chimneys. Continuing on an overall N bearing with the track, rise to contour left over the head of the valley towards the conspicuous, solitary, freestanding church of Saint Paraskevi (2). The track swings W through more olive groves, contouring and rising around the head of the side valley, above the valley of Vathi (3) that leads SW to and through the Stomio Gorge to the sea.

Continue towards the summit ridge outcrops ahead and above, on a 350° bearing for 75–100m (246–328ft), walking approximately N, before swinging left and ascending. Our route is now within the SW–W quadrant as we come to a gated enclosure that supports an animal pen. Note the fine views of Dikeos and the neighbouring summit of Plakoselia whose flanks run down to Vathi in the valley floor.

Walk W between two fences, then veer half-right, 10° E of S, by a solitary tree. On the left stands Saint Paraskevi, NE of which several mountains surrounding Tiflos Valley can be seen, including Oxo Koproula south

One of Inahorion's quaint chimneys

of Katsomatados. At an acute left-turn ahead, turn left, bearing 120°, through a gate, descending slightly, passing a crumbling *spilari* (shepherd and animal shelter) to the red pantiles and fading white walls of this Byzantine chapel. Below, a scatter of white-walled villages grace the green and fertile mountain enclave.

Return to the gate, noting the polite request in English, 'Please close the door'. Once through turn left, ascending W to approximately 750–800m (2461–2625ft), overlooking the head of Skotini Gorge at the abandoned village of Simadiriana. Rejoin, just left, our encircling head-of-valley track. A dirt and stone track, with its centre of grass/small flowers, journeys S, giving us an eagle's-eye view E over the valley floor into the hidden side valley of Tzitzifa.

Descend N and E, encircling another *spilari* before losing more height on an extensive series of U-bends. These zigzags obligingly provide ever-changing views N and S, before proceeding NNE in parallel to and above the now visible tarmac road to Papadiana.

Pass through a wiremesh gate and 25m beyond take the right fork, ignoring the concrete track on the left. Descending still, the way appears to come to a dead end as a track, and changes into a dirt/donkey pathway that leads into olive groves, vegetable patches and the occasional small vineyard. The zigzag pathway drops from tier to tier, overall N, at times between two stone walls, from where the road can be seen, below right. Continue to lose height, between shady platania and oleander, crossing a dried-up watercourse, with drinking trough, coming in from the left. Underfoot cement steps ease the passage onto the tarmac road below, before Papadiana.

Once onto the road veer left through the scattered houses, some old and abandoned, and the imposing roadside church of Panagia (Virgin Mary), as the road wriggles through N and E for a short, tree-lined, picturesque return to Kefali.

Items of Interest

(1) **NIKOLAOS PIMPLIS**, 1872–1963. A man of Kefali and Vathi, a Professor of Education and a great patriot in the 1941–45 German occupation, during which time he saved many of his fellow Cretans – men, women and children – from execution.

(2) **SAINT PARASKEVI**. Saint Paraskevi (Friday) has a red-pantiled roof with a semicircular protuberance at its east end (a hallmark of Byzantine churches). Inside is sadly in need of repair, especially the ceiling. From the church south and southeast we are looking over Vathi in the valley floor up to the enclave of Tzitzifa (Walks 31 and 33), on a bearing of 130°, in a side valley on the southwest flank of Plakoselia.

(3) **VALLEY OF VATHI AND STOMIO**. Scenically at its atmospheric best seen from Kefali, Tzitzifa and Louhia Col, when it displays a mix of weather – swirling hillside mist, brilliant sun's rays, black cloud over Stomio Gorge and early morning or evening light.

WALK 31

The Mountainous Enclave of Tzitzifa

Vathi, Tzitzifa, Plokamiana, Vathi

Distance	7.5km (4¾ miles)
Height Gain	250m (820ft)
Start/Finish	Vathi/Vathi
Grade	2–2½
Walking Time	3 hours
Maps	'Wanderkarte' KRETA Chania, 1:79,000
	harms IC verlag 1:100,000 Western Crete
	ISBN 3–927468–16–9
Accommodation	Kefali, and refreshments also in Vathi

A C-shaped walk if finishing in Plokamiana, a circular if returning to Vathi. Underfoot it varies from an ascending, asphalt country road, a descending dirt track, to a final section via a winding, undulating, tree-lined (mostly olive) dirt track along the valley floor from Plokamiana to Vathi. Overhead is a sky of spiralling raptors set against a backdrop of scrub- and rock-clad 1000m (9328ft) peaks. As the route is mainly above the tree line, spectacular and distant vistas can be enjoyed. This walk, dedicated to Krisoula, Dimitrios and Stomatis (see Acknowledgements at the beginning of the book), has everything – olive groves and cypress trees below, and mountain views, verdant valleys and mountain villages. An experience for those who seek solitude and new horizons, and for biologists, bird-lovers and those in search of yesterday.

The Route

Start from the war memorial by the large plane tree in Vathi's square. Descend S with the main road and at the junction ahead, signposted '← Tzitzifa 3km', leave the road left to cross a ford by a derelict, although recognizable, olive-oil mill (1), with remnants of presses, grindstones and machinery scattered within. Its crumbling state forbids inspection other than from the doorway. Continue with the narrow road crossing over the bridge above the musical, unnamed river.

Geraniums abound south of the river, and after the last of the houses (some of which are quite old) to the south, take the right fork with a tarmac surface. Ahead and below are the tidy church and cemetery SW of Vathi. Continue ascending and contouring on the olive-shaded road (not marked on maps) – a delightful journey S and SW, flanked with the occasional aloe cactus.

Note the picturesque hillside villages of Kefali and Papadiana (Walk 30) N, at the same elevation across the valley, or SW towards Stomio Gorge and the elongated village of Plokamiana. Higher now, still with the asphalt, weave S and W through more olives on a scrubby, nut-tree-lined roadway. W along the V of Stomio Gorge the conspicuous dome of yet another Profitas Ilias (site of Minoan sun worshippers) dominates the skyline above the sacred white walls of Monastery Chrisoskalitissis.

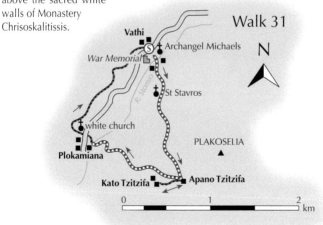

171

Himeos (Saint) Stavros and, beyond, Skotini Gorge

A small chapel, Himeos (Saint) Stavros, its pure white walls of pleasing proportions, catches the eye to the right, straddling a jutting spur. At the head of this tiered side valley, ascending SW, several old houses and cultivation terraces herald Kato (lower) Tzitzifa, and quicken the step to discover if Apano (upper) Tzitzifa lies hidden around the corner. In all my mountain wanderings, seldom have I experienced such pleasure and delight as on discovering this tiny village of six souls, tucked tight below Plakoselia 1013m (3324ft) and Tsounara 1105m (3626ft).

Leave Upper Tzitzifa, via the twisting road of entry for a short distance, to descend left, i.e. W, WSW then NW, first on tarmac then by dirt roads. Ignore side tracks, keeping to the wider track to Plokamiana. The zigzag descent eventually reaches and crosses the river. Ascend to the east end of the village, marked by a white church (Walk 32).

Cross the road just below the church onto a track, between church and buildings old and new, identified by an E4 long distance path waymark on the left. The narrowing track runs NNW with a tree- and shrub-covered ascending gully and watercourse. The half-hidden path, after 100m or so, opens out into a well-crafted, clearly visible pathway through the small gully, utilising resident stones for steps as it ascends.

Left of the path a compact stone wall acts as guide through the tiered olive groves. Ahead and above a communications mast can be seen W of the hillside village of Papadiana, as the old donkey trail steadily ascends to a T-junction straddling the 300m (984ft) contour. Here turn right onto a good 4WD track, E, for the final kilometre to Vathi. Initially descending, this almond-flanked way provides views of and above Tzitzifa and the church below, framed by pencil-thin cypress probing skywards. The curving track brings Vathi into view ahead, i.e. E. Below right is the modern olive press replacement for the derelict one seen below the square in Vathi.

Continue E to a very sharp U-bend, leaving the wide dirt track for an old donkey track into olive groves ahead. After a few metres join and walk E and N alongside a wiremesh fence on the right. Leave the stepped olive grove by a red-pantiled house. Fifteen metres ahead on the tarmac, by prickly pear and aloe cactus, a concrete stepped path descends right and winds its way into Vathi, where war memorial, giant platania, bus stop, and Tassos's bar, barber's shop and meeting place for all, grace the square.

Should you require transport, a morning bus, Kastelli–Elafonisos, arrives at Vathi at approximately 9.45am, returning from Elafonisos through Plokamiana at 4.15pm, then to Vathi, providing a choice of finishing the walk either at Plokamiana or Vathi.

Items of Interest

(1) **OLIVE OIL MILLS**. Homer referred to Crete as 'fair and prolific', capable of nourishing 'the golden tree' – the olive tree – which covers three-quarters of Crete's fertile land. This mainstay of the population provides nourishment, light, heat, cooking oil, fuel and building material. Olives are harvested in autumn and early winter and taken to be pressed (note the old millstones in the factory). The first two cold pressings produce a premium oil, subsequent hot water pressings provide oil for soap manufacture, while solid remains are mixed into animal feed or used as fertiliser.

WALK 32

The Plokamiana Loop

Plokamiana, Donkey Track North and West,
Lower Skotini Gorge, Plokamiana

Distance	3km (2 miles)
Height Gain	150m (492ft)
Start/Finish	Plokamiana/Plokamiana
Grade	2
Walking Time	1½–2hours
Maps	'Wanderkarte' KRETA Chania, 1:79,000
	harms IC verlag 1:100,000 Western Crete
	ISBN 3–927468–16–9
Accommodation	Rooms at Kefali, refreshment also in Vathi; a bus, Kastelli to Elafonisos, passes through, returning in the afternoon

A short stroll from, above and to Plokamiana with close ups of indigenous flora and fauna, coupled with instant isolation and windows of distant views. Underfoot, ascending and descending donkey tracks and grass and dirt tracks overlook Plokamiana and reveal the uninviting mouth of Skotini Gorge, before the return to Plokamiana.

The Route

Start from the east end of this elongated village, facing N, a white church and cemetery on the right, an E4 long distance trail waymark to the left, alongside buildings old and new. Here a narrow, tree- and shrub-covered dry watercourse ascends, a degree or so W of N. Initially narrow and half-hidden, the path after 100m or so opens out into a well-crafted, clearly visible, rising path through the narrow gully, utilising resident stones for steps.

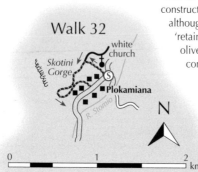

Walk 32

white church

Skotini Gorge

Plokamiana

R. Stomio

N

0   1   2 km

Left of our ascending path a well-constructed stone wall acts as guide, although its purpose is that of a 'retainer' for surrounding tiered olive groves. Ahead and above a communications mast can be seen W of the hillside village of Papadiana, as the old donkey trail, slabs underfoot and flanked with aloe cactus, comfortably zigzags ever upward, metre by metre.

Emerging, approximately on the 300m contour, at a dirt track junction, leave the donkey trail left, exchanging it for a rising, grass-centred track, running roughly S through several fields cloaking the descending shoulder above Plokamiana. The track rounds the shoulder W, 100m or so above the village, narrowing to a footpath. It's a section that provides appealing and extensive views (1) over the valley, S into the side valley of Tzitzifa. Continue swinging right, as if heading into Skotini Gorge below the abandoned village of Simadiriana – although in 2004 one village house appeared to be occupied.

On the left are several small neglected vines, while underfoot the path has narrowed and become overgrown, although still recognizable. Above, no olives or vines grow, as our now stony path descends to meet a T-junction. **Caution** – pebbly, pitted laval rock clutters the path through scrub and bushes. At the junction ahead swing left, i.e. SE, alongside a wire fence right of the descending pathway, into shady olive groves.

Underfoot the well-worn stone-stepped track confirms that this was the old pathway from Plokamiana to the empty mountain settlement of Simadiriana at the head of Skotini Gorge. This canny donkey track meanders down through the olives into a tidy patchwork of

fruit and vegetable gardens, by a concrete water tank, finally spilling into Plokamiana's only street, opposite the white walls and red pantiles of House Number 25.

Donkey trail to Plokamiana below the Skotini Gorge

Items of Interest
(1) **MOUNTAIN VIEWS**. East to south, beyond the lost village of Tzitzifa, the skyline is serrated by the coned and rounded summits of Kissamo's finest. From left to right, Plakoselia 1013m (3324ft), Dikeos 1184m (3885ft) and Tsounara 1105m (3626ft).

WALK 33

Pendihorion – Five Villages Walk

Kefali, Papadiana, Plokamiana, Tzitzifa, Vathi, Papadiana, Kefali

Distance	12km (7½ miles)
Height Gain	500m (1641ft)
Start/Finish	Kefali/Kefali
Grade	3
Walking Time	4½–5 hours
Maps	'Wanderkarte' KRETA Chania, 1:79,000 harms IC verlag 1:100,000 Western Crete ISBN 3–927468–16–9
Accommodation	Rooms and refreshment in Kefali, refreshments in Vathi; a bus, Kastelli to Elafonisos, passes by Kefali and through Vathi and Plokamiana, returning in the after noon (Easter to October)

This circular journey, through the picturesque municipality of Inahorion, visits and explores five villages that grace the hillsides and fertile valley floor of the Stomio/Vathi valley. Underfoot good paths, country lanes and old donkey tracks assist passage that is never too strenuous, yet gives varying views of mountain and valley. Don't forget your water bottle.

The Route

Kefali's taverna-lined thoroughfare, high on the valley's north ridge 575m (1887ft), provides grandstand views of the entire walk. Vathi or Plokamiana also provide a 'start/finish', as both are on the bus route. Walk W with the road that swings left at the tree-shaded statue of Professor Pimplis (1) by a children's playground. Follow this scenic road, overall W, via a series of looping

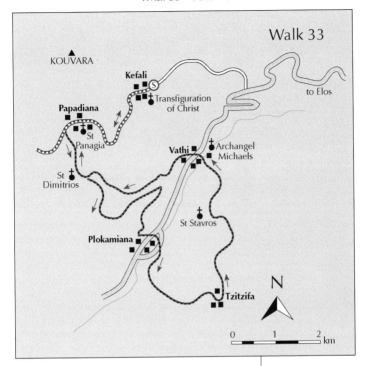

U-bends to Papadiana, a straggling village that clings to the upper northern ridge. It is a village with two churches, Panagia (Virgin Mary) of 1874, and the smaller Saint Dimitrios S of the village astride a sloping shoulder.

The road W crosses a bridge before entering the village. Note the ◁E4▷ European long distance trail waymarks that pass through several nearby villages en route to Elafonisos and Paleochora (Walks 34 and 36). Note also the unique house chimneys to the left. Pass 'dereliction corner' (2), W, to the final house, by a lampost, as the road swings right. Leave the road to descend left with a concrete track leading to the conspicuous Saint Dimitrios, on a south-facing shoulder.

The west end of Kefali

At the church swing around and take the right-hand track, N and then S on its east side, concreted, to a four-road junction below. Take the left one, concrete underfoot, that reveals Vathi below. The concrete peters out onto a descending stone and dirt track leading to an 'inverted Y' junction. Turn sharp right, walking more or less back on yourself, but at a lower level, SW, with olives and two cypress trees on your right. The track now leads around spurs and small gullies, surrounded by olives and in places almond lined (beehives on the right), walking a degree or so S of W.

There are now, left, fine views of Plakoselia 1013m (3324ft), the mountain dominating Tzitzifa. Pass a U-bend, covered in flowering oleander, descending E by a small turning space to a meeting of three tracks; ignore the one swinging E. Take the right-hand one, to descend through a water-gouged gully, stone and rocks on the right as you walk S. Aim for the distant Tzitzifa church on the hillside above, before swinging right, i.e. W, with the line of the valley floor. Ignore the next left fork on this coloured, wooded way SSE that swings and undulates W. The track now veers NW, meeting more beehives by a tree-filled gully on the left. The track is now lined with almond trees, and as it swings left crossing a dried-up watercourse – STOP.

The final leg to Plokamiana is immediately left, into the small narrow gully and watercourse descending by donkey track through flowers, scrub and olives to the church at the east end of Plokamiana (Walk 32). If you do not wish to go further, the returning bus to Kefali, Elos, etc., from Elafonisos passes through soon after 4pm (check current timetables). If the spirits are willing and the legs strong, leave the village at its east end by the church.

Cross the main road, church on the left, village on the right, to descend with the left fork of the road that bypasses below the south side of Plokamiana. Leave the road left and cross the river, to begin the 350m (1148ft) ascent to the fastness of Tzitzifa. The wide dirt road ascends via a series of long, but not exhausting, U-bends and zigzags that rise relentlessly SE, ENE and E towards Tzitzifa and its mountainous backdrop. Ignore small side tracks to meet with the tarmac road from Vathi. The abandoned agricultural buildings of Kato Tzitzifa are visible to the right. Turn right, passing solitary houses before the village clinging to the hillside ahead. Here stands Tzitzifa (3), and by the vociferous barking of the village dogs they know it too. After a rest and/or inspection of this centuries-old village, leave via the incoming tarmac lane.

When the ascending road from Plokamiana is met, coming in left, carry on descending NE into the picturesque, bountiful valley below. Feast your eyes on the white walls of Himeos (Saint) Stavros, and beyond into the Stomio and Skotini gorges. Don't miss the fine bank of pencil-thin, dramatic green cypress trees that grace the western approaches into Vathi. A descent to the riverside, a bridge crossing, a prowl around and a well-earned refreshment or a haircut in Tassos' *cafenion*/barber's shop/village store is recommended.

Leave the square, with its war memorial and giant platania, ascending the tarmac and concrete lane, via the western corner, with the post office and medical centre on the left. The lane changes to track, footpath and stepped way, emerging left by a red pantiled roof. A

Plokamiana squeezes into the valley floor

wiremesh fence on the left opens out through olive trees onto a sharp-angled dirt and stone U-bend, W of the last house above Vathi. At the U-bend take the ascending, right-hand track – it's a steady climb N.

Many tracks and paths crisscross the hillside below Papadiana, at times confusingly so. But there are two factors that aid navigation should my route descriptions fail to guide you to Papadiana. One, the conspicuous walls of Saint Dimitrios astride its spur, and two, when faced with a choice of tracks/paths, take the one that ascends. **To reach Papadiana you have to pass the Church of Saint Dimitrios.**

At the next fork turn right onto a new track rising N, initially between scrub and olives, then continue ascending NE toward Papadiana. Swing left now into the northern quadrant, with Papadiana directly ahead and above beyond the next junction. Take the left-hand rising track, veering right onto concrete to meet Saint Dimitrios (4), with its interesting cemetery and panoply of valley and mountain views.

From the church to Papadiana is a short step. Explore the village, with its narrow floral walkways between angled houses, to reach the imposing roadside Church of the Virgin Mary (Panagia). Beneath a venerable plane tree, it displays a fine engraved arch above its main door.

From Papadiana to Kefali (5) is a wriggling roadside stroll N and E, with enthralling views into this most pleasing of valleys, and fine sightings above to the NE.

Items of Interest

(1) **PROFESSOR PIMPLIS** 1872–1963. A local man, Professor of Education, hero and saviour of many – men women and children – during the 1941–45 German occupation of Crete. Statues of the Professor, in grateful appreciation from the peoples of Vathi and Kefali, stand in both villages.

(2) **DERELICTION CORNER**. A disaster waiting to happen at this S-bend and a nightmare for bus drivers (worse for passengers at the front). With only inches to spare, the front of today's buses hang over a considerable drop onto rooftops while manoeuvring around this intrusive, 'crumbling' corner of abandoned property.

(3) **TZITZIFA**. Ten British soldiers were hidden, undiscovered, in Tzitzifa roof space or in animal shelters during the Second World War. Electricity came in 1991, TV and the asphalt road from Vathi arrived seven years later.

(4) **SAINT DIMITRIOS**. Sitting high on its mountainside spur, this delightful church and its tidy cemetery provide not only fine vistas but also interesting facts about times gone by, not least the longevity of Papadiana's residents. A stroll through the cemetery reveals that the majority of occupants, if not all, lived well into their 80s or 90s, confirming their healthy diets and lifestyle.

(5) **KEFALI**. The Church of Transfiguration ('Metamorphosis') of Christ is Byzantine, circa 1320, and has a splendid example of wall-painting restoration. Note on the arched roof the painting of the nail holes in Christ's hands and feet.

WALK 34

Chrisoskalitissis to Elafonisos

*Chrisoskalitissis, the Wilderness, Bay, Lagoon
and Islands of Elafonisos*

Distance	10.5km (6½ miles)
Height Loss	50m (164ft)
Start/Finish	Chrisoskalitissis/Elafonisos
Grade	4
Walking Time	5 hours
Maps	'Wanderkarte' KRETA Chania, 1:79,000
	harms IC verlag 1:100,000 Western Crete
	ISBN 3–927468–16–9
Accommodation	Chrisoskalitissis and Elafonisos, plus refreshments; a morning bus,
	Kastelli to Elafonisos, passes through and returns at 4pm
Water	At least 2 litres per person in summer

This adventurous, linear windswept walk on Crete's southwest coastal extremity has much to offer. After an intriguing ecclesiastical start from Monasterie Chrisoskalitissis the walk goes south, between sky and sea, displaying a wealth of flora and fauna. Testing in sections, paint waymarks on stones and rocks are often hidden or faded, requiring a sharp eye, compass experience and the ability to recognise overgrown paths. This varied route provides interests to suit all. The finale at Elafonisos is coastal perfection in the minds of many, equalling Tigani in Balos Bay.

The Route
The Tavern Andiron, at the T-junction bus stop for Monastery Chrisoskalitissis, is a convenient starting point for this coastal walk, for not only are refreshments available, but also route information from the taverna's friendly proprietor. Walk W into the village from the bus

stop for approximately 300m, with the dominant and impressive white and cream walls of Monastery Chrisoskalitissis (1) astride a rocky promontory over-looking the blue waters of Stomio Bay. Pleasant houses and tidy olive groves bring us to a T-junction, leading right to the monastery and left for the road, track, path and then wilderness to Elafonisos.

Such is the appeal of this unique monastery, with its 'golden stair', that it attracts all. After inspection, return to the T-junction for a lengthy, in places unmarked wilderness trek S and SE. It requires a keen eye, ability to read a compass, and as paint waymarks vary in colour, the ability to distinguish different colours. In the midday heat of summer the walk is strenuous, although the rewards are high, visually and physically, when golden beaches, azure lagoons and the islands of Elafonisos are seen.

At the first-met T-junction note the arrowhead waymarks – orange, yellow and blue. Walk S, gardens right and ahead a fig tree growing out of what appears to be a well in the middle of the road, with a palm tree beyond; rise with the road to leave the village. At a crossroads cross and continue S, avoiding paths/tracks left or right. Note the individualistic chimneys, symbolic of the Municipality of Inahorion, as our track continues to wind. At the next crossroads, by houses and fenced gardens, an arrowhead and yellow–blue–red splodges

Walk 34

Chrisoskalitissis Monastery

Chrisoskalitissis

Lone house

Ruins

KEFALA

Elafonisos

Lagoon

Elafonisos island

N

0   1   2 km

185

Chrisoskalitissis Monastery

direct us over the crossroads, descending towards open country of scrub and rock on the seabound, i.e. W, sloping ridges ahead.

Cicadas scrape out a monotonous tune to the right, while to the left the shoreline belt of stony ridges rises E to a higher range of barren mountains that forms the great western bastions of Kefala and Vitsilia. Rock and conifer line our rising track, with a palm tree right displaying a splodge of red paint as the ridge ahead slopes seaward. We meet a forked junction, identified with coloured waymarks and a small, solitary house ahead. Take the track ahead, passing the house of 'one window, one door', continuing S, to ascend over the rocky brow. Tracks and paths join our route of yellow and blue spots, and at the next right-hand layby yet more splodges.

Underfoot the terrain is changing, becoming wild, deserted, scrub clad and rock strewn – not a place to experience wind storms or temperatures exceeding 40°C. Walk a degree or so either side of S, and at the next junction triple waymarks at a fenced area, left, direct us onto the right-hand fork (blue arrow) towards a wire fence at the lower sloping end of an E–W ridge.

Walk SW with the blue dots to cross the sloping ridge, beyond which proceed S, as the sea to the west reveals the mast-marked, west end of the finger of Elafonisos Island. At the next fork walk right and ahead, close by the few remains of habitation and animal shelters (2), beneath a tumble of water-washed and wind-worn overhanging rock. From here continue S and SE to pass through a gated wire fence, identified with a sprig of scrub and a wooden board, and on a large rock 5m beyond yellow, blue and orange waymarks. Beyond, frequent paint marks direct onto a narrow path through an ill-defined wilderness of stone and scrub for the next few kilometres.

Our SE and S route, rising through stone and scrub-clad desert, has one common denominator along the way, i.e. paint waymarks. Through this 'desert' section there are invariably orange splodges on sand-coloured rock, not easily seen, hence the previous warning to the colour-blind who trek alone. ▶

Continue through scrub and stone between 170°–180°. **As the thin trod frequently varies within the southbound quadrant, I include compass directions that relate to the presence of waymarks, now mainly orange or red, crossing this rock desert S. To describe each left and right would take longer than the walk!**

Passing 2m (6½ft) high weathered waymarked rocks, bearing 170°, head for a line of eye-catching rocks, also waymarked, on a thin trod that veers temporarily on 145°. When past, continue between 170°–180°. A larger outcrop, left, can be seen, and underfoot conditions improve as scrub gives way to short grass and stunted trees as we continue, bearing 180°, with the sea on our right hand. Make for a single, freestanding tree ahead – 175° – passing five small trees, still on the thin path (orange waymarks,) before the largest swing yet to 145°. Soon revert right to 160°, making for a clutch of larger rocky outcrops and stunted trees, passing between them and the sea. Conditions underfoot are much improved as we revert back to bearings between 165°–170°, ascending gradually towards a seat-like rock (orange

Another way to identify passage through this rock-strewn wilderness, south of the house ruins and animal shelters, is by compass as the narrow trod – orange or red waymarks – falls conveniently within the SE–S quadrant.

waymark) on large stepping stones, passing a series of rocky coves and inlets below. Don't attempt a scrambling descent!

Leave this attractive shoreline with waymarks, to swing left on a 120° bearing, contouring left towards a distinctive green tree ahead on a seabound shoulder. Our route is now between 125° and 130°, as we pass the 'umbrella' scrub oak and a line of stubbly conifers above rocky bays to reach clearer ground. Waymarks change to yellow and blue lines, small piles of stones, then red arrowheads by juniper trees. Ascending on bearings of 170°–175° on the shoulder rock, we are now rock-hopping, with care. As the scenery changes you can sense the approach of something spectacular ahead and below (3).

Arriving with orange and yellow-lined waymarks at a stepped way, through scrub – bearing 160° – a small rise ahead reveals a wide stone and dirt track. Orange and blue waymarks guide us on a thin trod – bearing 110° – through scrub, past a line of spiralled metal posts, on a line of waymarked stones swinging E onto the dirt track flanked to the north by an area of barren, sterile land.

Our route turns right, i.e. S, for a short distance to a T-junction. A few metres S of the junction takes the walker to the edge of the hill top providing, with care, an aerial view of the geographical/geological perfection that is Elafonisos. Return to the junction, descending E by a wide, sun-baked track that swings left and right with ever-changing and enlarging views of what lies below, and the mountains and sugarloaf rocky summits of the coastal hills.

Coastline, lagoon and island, the highlights of Elafonisos, lie below as we walk E. Tree-framed bays of clear blue water and extensive sands, with the western finger jutting into the Libyan Sea, are revealed as we approach on the waymarked, descending track to the tarmac road from Chrisoskalitissis. Turn right at the blue/yellow waymark onto the descending road, passing rooms, tavernas, *cafenion* and bars, leading to the lagoon

Elafonisos beach and lagoon

and warm waters. Take time to stroll, to explore, swim and enjoy the lagoon, island and village of Elafonisos.

There is a daily ferryboat (spring to autumn at 4pm) to Paleochora (Walk 36).

Items of Interest

(1) **MONASTERY CHRISOSKALITISSIS**. It is said that one of the 90 steps to the summit of the rock on which the monastery stands is a step of gold. Sinners, however, cannot see this golden step that gave the monastery its name – Chrisoskalitissis' ('Golden Stair'). Visitors are welcome to view church and s*aloni* (lounge and dining room). Its history is sketchy, original documents having perished through the ages, but not so this haven of hope that has withstood the aggressive invasions of Venetians, Turks, and more recently Germans. In the 1940s sections were converted into a prisoner of war camp.

(2) **OLD DWELLINGS AND ANIMAL SHELTERS**. Small, stone (undressed), angular houses and simple animal shelters with solid olive-wood lintels and low doorways.

(3) **ELAFONISOS SHIPWRECK** – 1907. On the island of Elafonisos, among the dunes and colourful flowers, stands a memorial to the Australian mariners of the SS *Imperatrice*, who perished in a shipwreck.

CHAPTER 3

Byzantine Selinos

THE AREA

The Principality of Selinos is fringed by the Libyan Sea on its southern shores and corralled to the east by the awesome mass of the Lefka Ori (White Mountains). Selinos' mountains, gorges and valleys are equally appealing though smaller in stature, and fine of form, providing the hill-walker with similar scenery, terrain and navigational challenges, albeit on a smaller scale. Biggest is not always best, for what Selinos lacks in height, bulk and degree of difficulty, it has in variety of terrain, variation of form and challenge, as well as many intriguing 'Items of Interest' along the way, including ecclesiastical highlights and a flourishing, colourful mix of flora and fauna.

It is an area of wild beauty, coupled with a turbulent history, and occupied by a race of proud and honourable people whose ancestors have seen invaders of many races come and go, yet the Cretan soul remains and predominates today. The countryside matches its inhabitants, and has a great deal to offer the pedestrian visitor who, on his or her journey, through on-foot adventures, can experience and learn much of the life and times of Selinos. One dominant influence on people and place was that of the Byzantine Period, when Christianity visually manifested itself in the churches throughout Selinos. Its beliefs are displayed in the classic paintings that can be seen on the internal walls and roofs in the majority of churches throughout the principality.

THE WALKS

The 11 walks, four from the coastal accommodation base of historic Paleochora and six from the resurgent city of Kandanos, explore the coastal surrounds from Paleochora and the seldom-visited high plateau and surrounding mountains of Kandanos.

Walk 35 is a circuit of Paleochora, providing a fascinating exploration into the life and times of this town of antiquity. It couples a town walk, with varying coastal and mountain views, with a rewarding ramble through time. **Walk 36** treads a coastal section of the ◁E4▷ long distance trail for an outstanding coastal, cliff top and hill walk from Paleochora or Cape Krios to Elafonisos. It requires care and attention underfoot for the experienced rock-hopper. The return to Paleochora via an inshore ferryboat makes this journey unique. **Walk 37**, entitled 'An Eagle's-eye View of Paleochora' is just that. A hill walk that ascends 350m (1148ft) north from Paleochora, with

A bird's-eye view of Paleochora
(Walks 35 and 38 as seen from Walk 37)

fine views of sea, coastline, mountains of many heights, colourful flora and fauna, herds of goats, and bird's-eye impressions of Paleochora and its sculptured peninsula. **Walk 38** continues the theme of adventure and fine views, visiting two gorges, one of which is the narrow Anidri Gorge, packed tight with boulders, tangled vegetation and a burbling stream. Further attractions are the village of Anidri, its 14th-century Byzantine church and a pebble and sandy beach.

Walk 39, a gentle, undulating stroll, highlights varied wooded groves, bird watching and flower identification, in addition to ecclesiastical and artistic exploration. **Walk 40** is a pleasing, far-sighted, leisurely walk from Kandanos, passing the old village of Koufalotos en route to the rocky outcrop of 'Preacher's Pulpit'. Although not waymarked, its tracks, paths and visible 'pulpit' ease navigation. **Walk 41** is a circular journey from Kandanos, physically easy and mentally stimulating.

This gem travels through centuries of Byzantine history – a cornerstone of Cretan culture. In contrast, **Walk 42** is a grandstand journey to the high ridges and surrounding mountains above Kandanos, overlooking not only the charismatic city but also the blue waters of the Libyan Sea. A delight in May, when colourful flowers catch the eye and the air is full of scents and soaring, singing birds. **Walk 43** to the mountain village of Spina, and beyond if desired, if treated as a there-and-back trek, is a serious undertaking, involving a journey of 22km (13¾ miles) and an overall height gain of 594m (1949ft). One of the highlights of the route is 'Spinatiko' – the gorge of Spina. **Walk 44** is a leisurely circular walk from Kandanos to Anisaraki to Kandanos, mainly via picturesque, centuries-old church and trade routes. **Walk 45**, the final walk, utilises an ancient trail, to be restored and waymarked, alongside and above the River Kakodikiano, from Kandanos to Plemeniana.

191

WALK 35

The Paleochora Circuit

*Ferryboat Jetty, Skala, Main Street, Saint Panagia,
Castro, Pachia Amo, New Harbour, Ferryboat Jetty*

Distance	3.6km (2¼ miles)
Height Gain	50m (164ft)
Start/Finish	Paleochora
Grade	1
Strolling Time	2 hours
Maps	EFSTATHIADIS 1:79,000 CHANIA ISBN 960 226 531 0
	harms IC verlag 1:100,000 Western Crete (includes E4)
	ISBN 3–927468–16–9
Accommodation	Paleochora – a wide selection, and refreshments

A fascinating exploration into ancient and modern Paleochora, a charismatic metropolis sitting astride a curving peninsula probing south into the Libyan Sea. Known centuries ago as Orina ('In the Mountains'), I much prefer its current name, literally 'Ancient Town or Place'. Its blend of several civilisations, coupled with varying coastal and mountain views, provides a rewarding ramble through time.

The Route

In Paleochora (1), start at the jetty for coastal ferryboats (to Elafonisos, Sfakia, Loutro, Roumeli and Sougia) below the ferryboat office, at the southern end of the pebble and stone beach (*chalikia*), known as East Beach ('Skala'). With the sea and formidable rocky breakwater on your right, walk N on Skala promenade towards the mountainous interior of Selinos. Left, inviting tavernas, bars, *cafenions* and accommodation cater for seasonal tourists.

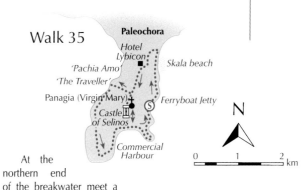

Walk 35

Paleochora

Hotel Lybicon

'Pachia Amo'
'The Traveller'

Skala beach

Panagia (Virgin Mary)

Ferryboat Jetty

Castle of Selinos

Commercial Harbour

N

0   1   2 km

At the northern end of the breakwater meet a pebbly (very) beach, proudly displaying its EC Blue Flag, between the tamarisk-lined promenade and the sea. The views east along the shoreline and mountainous coastline (Walk 38) reveal savage summits and seabound ridges above Sougia and beyond.

At 'Alexia, Rooms for Rent,' turn about, and at the first junction S turn right at Waves Taverna to cross, W, two streets running N and S, walking towards the conspicuous, fading remains (part renovated) of the one-time grand Hotel Lybicon ('Lyvicon') (2) on the main street. Turn left, walking S on the central thoroughfare – a road closed to vehicles from 7pm to 4am to enable residents and visitors to enjoy the thoroughfare free from speeding cars and motorbikes.

Continue S, bus station left and Dionysos Restaurant right. (Note several right turns, W, signposted 'To the Beach', known as Pachia Amo – we visit this delightful bay later.) Continue S towards the impressive towered church at the southern end of the street of varied shops, mainly to tempt the tourist, below the war-torn embattlements of Selino Kastelli (3). Pass on the right the Town Hall and its neighbouring municipal offices, fronted by an impressive statue of a Cretan military hero, Konstantin Kriaris, 1825–69 (4), an inspirational Selinos leader. Ahead stands the renovated principal church, Annunciation (1914). Pass by on the ascending pathway to the Castel del Selino of the Venetians.

The castle ruins, a fine grandstand looking over Paleochora, crown this small peninsula. After a full inspection of castle and views N, E and W of the hinterland of Selinos, plus S over the Libyan Sea to the island of Gavdos, return to the church. Continue past the church and at the first crossroads turn left, walking W for a short distance to the glorious sands of West Beach, (Pachia Amo), marked by a sculpture, 'The Traveller', by Bob Bunck (5).

Leave the bay S to rise and join the road S, i.e. right, that encircles the fort, to reach the area known as Tigani ('a pan and handle'), today an expanding commercial harbour (a modern, EU-funded development of boatyards and boats, including the Gavdos ferry). Continue E, now between Castro (castle), left, and the new harbour, right, to eventually rejoin the eastern promenade, breakwater and ferryboat jetty north of a rocky stretch of spectacular shoreline, past the Water's Edge Café, to return to the starting point at the ferry jetty.

Items of Interest

(1) **PALEOCHORA**. The town grew on the peninsula during the second half of the 1800s. It rose from the remains of ancient Kalamidi (the harbour for the old town of Kandanos). On the heights of its prominent peninsula the 13th-century conquering Venetians built Kastello Selino, giving the name 'Selinos' to the district. The castle was to fall, rise and fall again under the yoke of Venetians, Turks, the Algerian pirate Barbarossa, Cretan nationalists and Germans (1941–45). The basics of the town we see today developed in the latter half of the 19th century, exploding after the Second World War as a result of mass tourism.

(2) **HOTEL LYBICON**. This dominant three-storey building, built in 1935, stands at what was the northern end of the main street, before the explosion of tourism and the expansion of the town (there are now in excess of 3500 beds available). Since the disastrous 1941–45

conflict the Lybicon has slipped into decline, but in 2004 renovation began, although not as an hotel.

(3) **SELINO KASTELLI**. The remains of Kastello Selino (Castle of Selinos, 'the Fortezza'), built in 1280–82 by the conquering Venetians, straddling the highest point of the peninsula, command extensive views over the 'modern town' to the mountains beyond. Since its conception five nations have occupied the castle, the most oppressive being the Venetians, 1210–1450s, the Turks, 1669–1930, and Germans, 1941–45. Four times it has been resurrected. The remains today include the quadrangular enclosure – repaired by the Turks – several water-holding reservoirs/cisterns, and bits and pieces of buildings and dwellings. Best visited at sunrise or sunset for dramatic camera shots of town, surrounding sea and mountains.

(4) **KONSTANTIN KRIARIS 1825–69**. Kriaris masterminded the Cretan 'Selinos Uprisings' against the Turks. Born into a family of 'freedom fighters', he followed his father, Georgios, who fought alongside the revered Sfakiat, 'Daskalojannis'. Kriaris was in turn followed by his two sons – Aristides, who fought for freedom in the 1878–1896 conflicts, and Panajotis, historian and author.

(5) **'THE TRAVELLER'**. This sculpture is on the Pachia Amo promenade alongside the sandy bay on Paleochora's western shoreline. 'Unveiled 01-10-1992 by Stavros Likisaligakis, Mayor of Paleochora. This work was created by and offered to the people of Paleochora by the Dutchman, Bob Bunck, and friends. It symbolises the friendship between this 'village' and Travellers who have been visiting this place for years.' The man on the donkey and he who follows bring to mind Don Quixote and his manservant.

WALK 36

Crete's Southwest Extremity

*Shistonissi Bay (Cape Krios), 'Vienna',
Saint Ioannis, Elafonisos*

Distance	12km (7½ miles)
Height Gain	200m (656ft)
Start/Finish	Cape Krios/Elafonisos
Grade	4 (high exposure)
Walking Time	4½ – 5 hours
Maps	EFSTATHIADIS 1:79,000 CHANIA ISBN 960 226 531 0
	harms IC verlag 1:100,000 Western Crete (includes E4)
	ISBN 3–927468–16–9
Accommodation	Paleochora, Gialos, Elafonisos; also refreshments

An outstanding coastal, cliff-top and hill walk via a picturesque section of the ◁E4▷ long distance walk. The views, extensive and unique, complement a colourful and diverse flora and fauna. Other variables can be altered or adjusted to suit the walker's preferences, e.g. by starting from Elafonisos, Paleochora or Cape Krios. Paleochora adds 8km (5 miles) through or close to the centre of *thermokypra* – greenhouse tomato and cucumber production in Crete. After completing the walk, take the afternoon Elafonisos ferryboat back to Paleochora (check timetables). The walk, not to be rushed, demands care underfoot. It is for the experienced, well-equipped rock-hopper who can handle dehydration, heat exhaustion, and rocky sections of high exposure.

The Route
Start by walking W from the sandy beach of Shistonissi Bay, Crete's southwest extremity, before winding NW around the prominent rocky spur of Akrotiri (Cape) Krios. Look out for the waymarks of the ◁E4▷ (1) (yellow

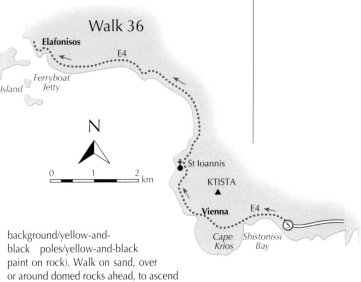

background/yellow-and-
black   poles/yellow-and-black
paint on rock). Walk on sand, over
or around domed rocks ahead, to ascend
W via a waymarked narrow zigzag, in places
quite steep, to join a wide dirt track. Turn left onto the
rising track to the col ahead. Over the col leave the track
for a narrow descending path, W, over the scrubby flanks
of Krios to enter a tree-clad, waymarked zigzag that leads
towards the cairned shoreline. Turn right onto a pebble
pathway to sheltered Ktista Bay and the remains of
Vienna (2), an ancient harbour whose outcrops of rock
W and N provide the harbour walls. Note the marble
remains strewn over the beach; here is a place to pause
and think of civilisations past.

Leave N and NW, on a steadily ascending stone-scat-
tered dirt path, with Ktista hill rising to 183m (600ft) on
our right, above the glistening waters of the Libyan Sea.

**Heed well where you put your feet, as high
exposure lies ahead**. The path passes very close to an
exposed rim of the cliff top, on your left, shown
correctly on EFSTATHIADIS 1:79,000 map, but not on
harms IC verlag 1:100,000 map. The troublesome few

197

Vienna's marble columns

metres of pathway, lying below four conical rocky outcrops, slope seawards towards the exposed rim of what appears to be a 75–100m (246–328ft) sheer cliff. The traverse of several metres of exposed path is not improved by the presence of small unstable stones. Walking poles would assist a stable crossing. Should you feel uncertain negotiating the 12m or so, or if troubled with vertigo, do not attempt the exposed path. Scramble a few metres above, and with hands and feet loop above and around the troublesome section. If you are not comfortable with the loop scramble, turn around and return to Shistonissi Bay via the outward path.

Ahead the northerly path leaves the cliff edges to veer right, contouring the spurs and shoulders that slope towards the sea, gradually descending to the solitary white church of Saint Ioannis (Saint John) (3) visible ahead. The church was locked, but it did provide shade, a seat and an interesting bell. From here Elafonisos can be seen to the northwest. Return to the track junction above the church to walk N and descend into the sand and rock bay.

The marked shoreline route, shown on harms IC verlag 1:100,000 map, runs N and NW, overlooked to the east by two unnamed summits, for approximately 2km (1¼ miles). Ascend sharply from the bay on an unstable path of stones and sand, which may require the use of hands, eventually leading into and out of a narrow gully incised into the rising hillside. With rock and sand underfoot, scrub and wind-blown trees around, the waymarks guide onto the shore, walking W, at times on rock slabs. Ahead waymarks continue to guide through an interesting mix of loose, sandy dunes covered by a scatter of wind-blown, contorted cypress and yew trees.

With sandy dunes and twisted conifers now behind, rock and scrub are our companions as the ◁E4▷ signs guide us NNW and W, in and out of the stony bays and inlets adorning this indented coastline, leading to the unlikely natural (read 'rocky') anchorage of 'm/v Elafonisos' (in 2003, 4.25 euros to Paleochora). If time allows, stroll W to explore, swim in and enjoy the lagoon, island (4) and village of Elafonisos. The boat returns at 4pm to Paleochora.

St Ioannis looks over the Libyan Sea to Elafonisos

Items of Interest

(1) **E4 – EUROPEAN TREKKING ROUTE**. The E4 begins its Cretan journey in Kastelli, passing through Kissamos and Selinos, an appropriate final lap for such a marathon. It winds its scenic and challenging way via Polyrinia, Lousakies, Sfinari, Kambos, Kefali, Vathi, Chrisoskalitissis, Elafonisos, Paleochora and Pavlos Beach, ending on Crete's eastern extremities.

(2) **VIENNA**. This ancient Dorian city and natural harbour is said to have been populated by Dorians from France. Note the remains of cylindrical marble columns littering the sands, approximately 0.61m (2ft) in diameter and 2m (6½ft) long; also two lines of large stones running 20m (66ft), 2m (6½ft) apart, to the water's edge. What became of this Dorian city remains a mystery.

(3) **SAINT IOANNIS**. The freestanding 1972 bell, cast in Chania, depicts in bas relief what I presume to be 'St Gorgeos' slaying the dragon, plus two saints beneath a T. One must surely be Saint John.

(4) **ELAFONISOS MASSACRE – 1824**. Women, children and 40 armed men were hiding on the 'island', awaiting a boat to transport them to the Ionian islands, beyond the reach of the occupying Turks. Unfortunately one Turk knew of the neck of land that connected island to mainland at low tide, and at the appropriate time led the invaders across. Eight hundred and fifty Cretans were slaughtered that Easter Sunday, remembered every year at the Elafonisos Feast.

WALK 37

An Eagle's-eye View of Paleochora

Paleochora, North to Panorama, Beyond the
Communications Mast on Wigles, Paleochora

Distance	6.5km (4 miles)
Height Gain	350m (1148ft)
Start/Finish	Paleochora
Grade	3
Walking Time	4 hours
Maps	EFSTATHIADIS 1:79,000 CHANIA ISBN 960 226 531 0
	harms IC verlag 1:100,000 Western Crete (includes E4)
	ISBN 3–927468–16–9
Accommodation	Paleochora; also refreshments

An ascending walk that initially taxes the lungs, but physical burdens are
soon forgotten as views of sea and coastline, mountains great and small,
colourful flora and fauna – including nifty goats – bird's-eye impressions of
Paleochora and its sculptured peninsula unfold. This is followed by a short
wildwalk, requiring compass work and common sense, that reveals much
of Selinos. With little or no shelter from the sun, nor water en route, take a
full water bottle, hat and sun cream.

The Route
The starting gate for this walk from Paleochora (1) stands
at the eastern corner of the highest, most northerly
(recently built) residential estate, Panorama. Easily reached
either from the main street N, then left, i.e. W, on the
Koudoura road, to the triple junction signposted 'Chania,
Voutas, Koudoura', **or** from the West Beach, walking with
the promenade N, gradually ascending N and E with the
Chania road to the signposted triple junction.

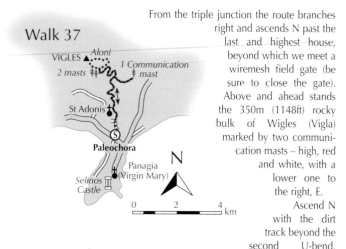

Walk 37

VIGLES ▲ *Aloni*

2 masts ‡‡ / 1 Communication ‡ mast

St Adonis ✝

Ⓢ
Paleochora

N

Panagia ‡ (Virgin Mary)

Selinos 🏛 Castle

0   2   4 km

From the triple junction the route branches right and ascends N past the last and highest house, beyond which we meet a wiremesh field gate (be sure to close the gate). Above and ahead stands the 350m (1148ft) rocky bulk of Wigles (Vigla) marked by two communication masts – high, red and white, with a lower one to the right, E.

Ascend N with the dirt track beyond the second U-bend, noting to the west, left, the small church of Saint Adonis perched on a tiered hillside, and the attractive probing finger of Akrotiri (Cape) Trahili poking S into the Libyan Sea. Note also the 32 sq km (12⅓ sq miles) of the island of Gavdos (2) some 32km (20 miles) SE from Paleochora. Our route zigzags, overall N, as height is rapidly gained. Look S to the ever-pleasing, expanding curved peninsula of Paleochora, its harbour at the tip, its pastel-shaded angular buildings and crumbling Kastelli Selinou. Pass large water tanks on the left as the flower-lined track, concreted on the acute bends, relentlessly weaves its ascending way towards the col above.

As the col is reached, walking E, note the ridges and summits of the ranges (3) to the east that plunge dramatically into the restless waters of the Libyan Sea. At the T-junction ahead, above an olive grove to the east, take the right fork to ascend to the single mast (seen from the West Beach) via a broad track.

Thirty-five minutes of visual pleasure has brought us to the single, lower red-and-white tower (4), and what views it provides, including further aerial sightings of the scimitar-shaped peninsula. **A word of warning – the**

summit exposure is severe in places. Return to the T-junction via the bare earth of the olive grove to ascend to two red-and-white masts, on a series of easy concrete, dirt and stone zigzags NW then W, then N overall. Paleochora comes into view again, and E are the angular greenhouses of Anidri (Walk 38), plus the church-capped hill SW of Anidri. Also clearly visible are the twists and turns of the Paleochora-to-Kandanos road, the deep-gouged valleys and gorges of the Kakodikianos river, and the dark fastness NW of the valley of Pelekaniotikos to Voutas.

A few metres below the towers, at the last wooden electric pole, leave the track to walk N on goat tracks, through and over low scrub between rocky outcrops. The route soon levels out, relatively speaking, onto a moon-scape plateau of upland scrub with outcrops of wind and water-fashioned sandstone, and in places what appears (to a non-geologist) to be laval rock. We are now on the ridge N and NW of the two masts – underfoot the low scrub is lacerated by goat tracks. Flowers of strong-smelling lavender abound as we walk NW, skirting N of the first large outcrop (avoid the southern aspects of the outcrops, as they fall rapidly into the valley below).

Aloni (winnowing circle) beyond Vigla

After passing the second outcrop make for small outcrops ahead, 183m to the west, 'cairned' by loose rocks, with, on your right, the occasional stunted tree. Notice on the left, i.e. S, 46–55m or so away, three flat stones atop each other – **avoid, as this rough ground spills dramatically S into a corrie below**. Look W and note a patch of bare earth 274/366m on a magnetic bearing of 300°. Pick your way towards the bare earth and before it veer right, making for a lower plateau, on a bearing of 320°, with scrub and 2m (6½ft) high olives trees – some close to death due to lack of water.

We are now on bare earth, surrounded by hills of exposed rock, in places split asunder by deep valleys on whose northwestern slopes isolated houses cling. Observe, on a bearing of 330°, a valley left, and as you walk towards the valley note underfoot an *aloni* (5) – a circle of flat, earthbound stones rising 46cm (18in) above the ground. From this point you can see the summit E of Gingilos – bearing 80° – and also the Anidri walk (Walk 38).

Walk E from the *aloni* towards a sharp-towered outcrop, and when reached veer half-right. Make your way back to the twin-towered hillock via a small ridge, walking overall S to meet the outcrops of the outward journey that led to the *aloni*. When the small outcrops, capped with stones, are met, swing left, i.e. E, through low scrub. Ahead stand the twin towers. Walk via the outward path to emerge at the track by the wooden electric pole below the twin masts.

From this point it is downhill to Paleochora. The track may be the same, but the views are not, although still of a high calibre and overall more distant.

Items of Interest

(1) **PALEOCHORA**. Known centuries ago as Orina, meaning 'In the Mountains', I prefer its current name, Paleochora, literally 'Ancient Town or Place'.

(2) **GAVDOS**. Administered by Selinos since 1942, this small island floating in the Libyan Sea lies 32km (20

miles) east of Paleochora, and in many ways is a topo-
graphical miniature of Crete. A harmonious island, clad
by coniferous and deciduous trees, it is home to around
50 islanders, reputed to be 'nature's gentlemen'.

(3) The 'crocodile head' of Pidaraki, 362m (1188ft),
hides Sougia beyond, north of which rise the giant western outlyers of the Lefka Ori – Pslifi 1984m (6510ft),
Gingilos 2080m (6824ft) and Volakias 2116m (6943ft).

(4) **COMMUNICATIONS MASTS**. In this high-tech age
these red-and-white masts are ever present on the high
ground of Western Crete. On the two sites the single
mast stands at 300m (984ft) and the twin masts at 350m
(1148ft). One plus for the walker is that the track to the
mountain top assists passage and provides views to the
west that include Akrotiri Krios, the southwest extremity
of Crete.

(5) *ALONI*. The *aloni* is a circle, approximately 9m (30ft)
across, enclosed by flat stones, earthbound on their thin
edge, rising approximately 46cm (18in) above the
ground. The hard floor of this circle comprises earth and
animal dung. Harvested grain to be winnowed
(threshed) was placed in a heap in an *aloni* situated on
high ground on a plateau, ridge or shoulder. To separate
the grain from the chaff, shovelsful (wooden paddles)
would be thrown into the wind – preferably a north
wind. The heavier grains fall back into the *aloni*, the
light chaff is blown away.

WALK 38

Paleochora, Two Gorges,

Anidri and the Sea

Paleochora, Azogires Gorge, Anidros, Anidri
Gorge, Pavlos Beach, Paleochora

Distance	12km (7½ miles)
Height Gain	300m (820ft)
Start/Finish	'Lybicon' on Paleochora's main street
Grade	3
Walking Time	5 hours
Maps	EFSTATHIADIS 1:79,000 CHANIA ISBN 960 226 531 0
	harms IC verlag 1:100,000 Western Crete (includes E4)
	ISBN 3–927468–16–9
Accommodation	Paleochora – wide selection and Campsites

Paleochora – fought over, knocked down and built again – provides an ideal start and finish for this seashore, two-gorge 'lollipop' walk. Underfoot are tarmac, stone and dirt, and sand and pebble roads, tracks and paths, with a scrambled descent on a boulder-strewn stream flanked by tangled vegetation within the Anidri Gorge. Plus, if you wish, a sand/pebble beach walk. Don't miss the extraordinary 14th-century Byzantine Church of Saint Georgios in Anidri. Sections of this walk are an arboreal delight.

Note On the EFSTATHIADIS map, the village north of Anidri is named Asfendiles. In the harms IC verlag map it is referred to as Azogires. In the text I use Azogires.

The Route

At the northern quarter of Paleochora's (1) main street stands the town's first, and what was its grandest hotel,

the Lybicon. The building is being restored, but not as an hotel. Here we start, initially following the frequent signs and directional N and NE markers, at street junctions, for the campsite. The floral route passes E4 waymarks and the town's distinct cemetery, and later, beyond the coastal olive groves, Paleochora Camping Club. One kilometre (⅔ mile) from Paleochora pass the caravans and tents of the camping club before meeting the Azogirianos river at the junction of our outward and inward route, beyond a fork in the tarmac lane. Pause awhile to look back along the beach to the appealing township and peninsula of Paleochora.

Turn left and take the left fork, N and NE, passing on the right the attractive Olive Tree holiday cottages, after the sign 'Anidri – left, Pavlos – right'. Ascend steadily NE and N through the Azogirianos Gorge for approximately 4km (2½ miles) on the twisting tarmac. The route goes between and beneath awesome tree- and scrub-clad cliffs at whose feet lie enormous blocks of rock, some the size of a house. Ascend between the ominous cliffs on the snaking road with the plunging, noisy, white-water river submerging and remerging at every turn, while birdsong bounces off the gorge walls.

As height is gained, looping SE and NE, leave the confines of this gorge as it continues N and NNE to

*Saint Georgios'
bell tower*

Azogires; our 4m (13ft) wide road wriggles NE, N and finally E through less severe ascents. Swing right at a water pumping station to meet and pass two angular, sand-coloured 'Ecological Guest Houses', E of which rears a great cliff of naked rock, farm buildings and plastic tomato houses. Our lane leads to a U-bend with adjoining barrier.

At this point, approximately 1 hour from Paleochora, leave the tarmac road to follow the dirt track/trod E (red dots and occasional '→' on rocks) through a series of tiered olive groves, overall E. On our left a dried-up waterbed, to the right olive groves. Rise gradually, making for the distinct conical, rocky summit of the hill ahead, as the path leads to the col on the N side of the summit, beyond which, to the east, nestles Anidri village.

Continue E with the guiding dots, and as you meet a wire fence the path forks – take the right fork, ascending two tiers, swinging right as the second tier, in between two close-growing olive trees, swings S on a thin path through sage and thistle. A wire fence on the right and a dot on a stone, left, guides you into an ascending, dried-up watercourse that leads, after a short distance, to a small cairn (pile of stones on rocks), where it spills onto a wide stone and dirt track at a Y-junction. Swing left, i.e. N, with an angular greenhouse immediately ahead. Fine mountain views fill the horizons as the good track, concrete in places, winds E, ascending slightly to join the tarmacked Anidri road below the tomato houses.

Turn right for the final metres leading into the floral village of Anidri (2), passing below the rocky northern summit of Papoura, on the right. Ringed by conical rocky peaks and cradled by flourishing olive groves, Anidri is blessed by the tiny, double-doored Church of Saint Georgios (3).

Central to the village is the *cafenion,* Sto Scolio – the Old School – from where, beneath a shady olive tree, views of the blue Libyan Sea unfold S between high hills. A few steps below the *cafenion* stands the Church of Saint Georgios. It would be a sin not to quietly enter and admire the extraordinary murals gracing the walls and domed ceilings.

Leave the village S from the church – signed 'To the Beach' – on a waymarked (blue arrowheads and words) zigzag that directs the ever-narrowing descent into Anidri Gorge. For 1.5km (1 mile) of sheer delight, within the southern quadrant, our route wriggles between rock and water as the trod crisscrosses the occasionally disap-pearing stream. Rock scrambling experience is advantageous, as are walking poles, at three points of concentrated big boulders. Raptors circle and screech above this tight, scrub-clad gorge, which obscures distant views until sea and beach *cantina* are finally spotted beyond Pavlos beach.

Rock-filled Anidri Gorge

Cantina and sea may tempt, but if not, turn right at the southern exit of the gorge for a pleasing shoreline 3.5km (2¼ mile) hike W. Initially the shoreline track returning to Paleochora is a mixture of dirt and sand, beneath the southern sun-baked flanks of Papoura (sections are utilised by the E4). The walk is now easy and open, providing a plethora of sea and shore views. One, close at hand, emphasises the perverse vagaries of nature, where she appears to have turned her priorities upside down. The beach, i.e. land adjacent to the sea, is composed of stones and pebbles, while the skirts of the hills rising from the shoreline are a mass of rock-studded sand dunes.

Continue W to reach and cross the Azogirianos river by bridge, to meet the outward path below the Olive Tree holiday cottages. This is followed WSW and SW, via Paleochora Camping Club, en route to Paleochora.

Items of Interest

(1) **PALEOCHORA**. Growing and prospering, Paleochora is high on the 'must go' lists of world travellers, as expressed by the 'Traveller' sculpture by Bob Bunck on the promenade overlooking the town's west beach.

(2) **ANIDRI**. It is said that the entire population of this small village had the same name, 'Vardoulakis', all being direct descendants of two Sfakiot brothers who, to evade a blood feud, fled to this remote, hidden plateau.

(3) **SAINT GEORGIOS**. A remarkable, two-doored restored (desecrated by the Turks) 14th-century Byzantine church dedicated to Saint George. Its domed roof bears an extraordinary wall painting by Joannis Pagomenos, depicting Saint George slaying a dragon, circa 1323, one of a collection of fascinating murals that equal masterpieces decorating the walls of Saint Marina (Walk 4).

WALK 39

Saint Kyriaki

*Kandanos, Saint Catherine, Saint Kyriaki,
Labiriana, Kandanos*

Distance	5km (3 miles)
Height Gain	100m (328ft)
Start/Finish	Kandanos, Saint Catherine
Grade	1
Strolling Time	2–2½ hours
Maps	EFSTATHIADIS 1:79,000 CHANIA ISBN 960 226 531 0
	harms IC verlag 1:100,000 Western Crete (includes E4)
	ISBN 3–927468–16–9
Accommodation	Apartments (limited); (authorities actively pursuing rooms to rent)

Should your outdoor interests include gentle, undulating scenic strolls through varied wooded groves, ecclesiastic and artistic exploration, bird watching and flower identification under blue skies and a Mediterranean sun, with a selection of refreshments at the end of the journey, then this walk is for you.

The Route

Start from Kandanos' (1) tiny roadside Church of Saint Catherine (2) below and E of the prominent Cathedral of the Ascencion. The road, with this externally restored church and several new buildings on the left, travels due S, presenting interesting views through an avenue of olives, to the ridges and summits of several 1000m mountains.

This first section, waymarked with a yellow arrowhead → 'Saint Kyriaki', takes us via tarmac lanes, an old donkey track and stone and dirt lanes/tracks between olive groves, sweet chestnut and giant platania. With the waymarks, pass on your left the pink-and-red roses of House Number 125. 30m beyond, at a right-angle bend in the lane, leave it to ascend with a narrow, stone-stepped donkey track that cuts out a lengthy U-bend on the lane.

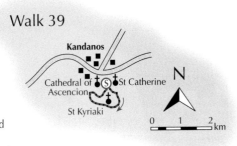

Emerge to rejoin the lane, and continue with the shaded tarmac, passing scented roses and silver-green olives. After crossing a bridge over a stream, flanked by colourful broadleaves, including walnuts, passing farm buildings and a house, the red pantiles of Kyriaki can be seen ahead. Concrete and dirt and stone tracks/lanes guide us W to a fork. Follow the signed arrow right to Saint Kyriaki (3), a Byzantine chapel in the district of Labiriana, reached after a 30 minute, 2km (1¼ mile) walk. Cretan churches have 'pathways' connecting them to neighbouring churches, villages and towns.

Kandanos – Cathedral of the Ascension and the Town Hall

213

St Kyriaki, Labiriana

Inspect the wall paintings within, and enjoy the extensive, pleasing and varied 360° views without, such as Apopigadi 1331m (4367ft), twin-peaked Vigla 1234m (4049ft) towering over Spina (Walk 43) rising to the NE, and distant Dikeos 1008m (3307ft) (Walk 25), dominating the western horizon. Leave Saint Kyriaki, with its west-end nameplate, to descend gradually NW and W, via a stone and grass track, for the return to Kandanos. The way is fenced on the right, i.e. above the gully; the views over this gully are of a sea of olive green sprinkled with red-pantiled and white-walled buildings.

The twin towers of Kandanos Cathedral are also conspicuous as we continue to descend WNW, i.e. overall NW, on the shaded dirt and stone track. Ahead, approach and pass through an extensive copse of stately oak and gaze over this garden of olive groves. Veering W toward the saucer's enclosing rim, note the immediate valley below to the west, the hillside Church of Prophet Elias, and some distance NE, on the valley floor, the detached bell arch of pantiled Saint Iannis (both Walk 41). Overhead, large black birds of prey (4) circle hungrily.

Beyond the copse of oaks note the flat-roofed house below. A zigzag descent left, right and left again, from an old *aloni* – a grain-winnowing circle with perimeter stones – passes the flat-roofed house, and several more, before swinging right onto a broad, descending road, concrete in places, tarmac in others, on a 10° variation of E to drop into the fertile valley floor. The road is surrounded by oak, and later ivy-infested giant plane trees – girth of 3–4m (10–13ft) (4) – as it winds E through this garden of hazel, *moura*, roses, walnuts, cherry, orange, apple, pear, cypress, and of course olive, as ancient and modern farms are passed.

Walk N, and as House Number 109 is passed walk E, i.e. right, with sightings ahead of Koufalotos' octagonal church tower from a cleared area of cultivated flat land on the left, leading to a road junction (with a Saint Kyriaki waymark indicating our outward route). Turn left over a watercourse for a short walk, overall N, along the floral, house- and garden-lined way to Saint Catherine's and Kandanos town centre.

Items of Interest

(1) **KANDANOS**. Kandanos has seen many friends and foes come and go through the last two millennia – Romans, Venetians, Turks and Nazi Germans. The last three fall into the latter category. It was as a result of the Nazi Germans' 'to-the-ground' policy of destruction during the Second World War that in 1989 Kandanos, the capital of Selinos, was honourably recognised as a city (reference the illustrated work *The Byzantine Churches of Kandanos*, published 1999, 'Kantania').

(2) **SAINT CATHERINE**. A recent exterior restoration, as this church had been destroyed, with only a few crumbling wall paintings surviving. Only two remain clear, a frieze of decorative tiles and *The Donor's Inscription*.

(3) **SAINT KYRIAKI**. The main church of the district (marble graves surround the church) presents an impressive picture of white walls and red-pantiled roof. Wall

paintings created in the first half of the 14th century, from 1305, have in the main been destroyed. The most distinct of the survivors is haloed Saint Panteleimon.

(4) **FLORA AND FAUNA**. Giant plane and wild sweet chestnut trees hugging watercourses and upland streams are often embraced by thick tendons of ivy – *Herbera helix*, a parasite carried from Asia into Europe by the god Dionysus, according to mythology. However, this prominent parasite has its good points, in spite of its toxic fruit, as a tincture of ivy leaves successfully treats burns, and its wood is in demand by artisans who craft the Cretan lyre.

There are more than 40 differing species of birds, the majority being resident, a lesser number migratory. The most easily recognized are spectacular raptors – vultures and eagles that soar on passing thermals, over high ridges and mountains, eyeing exhausted hillwalkers! One day, high above Bambakados (Vamvakados) and Temenia, while I was gazing south over Anidri into the Libyan Sea, a large eagle glided overhead eastward for some 366m without a single flap of its wings, with no apparent wind or breeze. Would that I could walk as eagles glide.

WALK 40

To 'Preacher's Pulpit'

*Kandanos, Koufalotos, Old Koufalotos,
'Preacher's Pulpit', Kandanos*

Distance	5km (3 miles)
Height Gain	150m (590ft)
Start/Finish	Kandanos
Grade	2
Walking Time	2 hours
Maps	EFSTATHIADIS 1:79,000 CHANIA ISBN 960 226 531 0
	harms IC verlag 1:100,000 Western Crete (includes E4)
	ISBN 3–927468–16–9
Accommodation	Kandanos – apartments (limited)

A relatively short walk, ideal as an introduction to charismatic Kandanos and its surrounds. Underfoot tarmac then dirt roads, and thin paths/trods through scrub – no waymarks. As height is gained views unfold and birds of prey fill the skies, and from April to June the hillsides are a mass of colourful flowers.

The Route

Walk E along the main street of lively Kandanos (1) with the twin towers of the cathedral behind. Beyond the baker's, the shops and dwellings dwindle as a T-junction is met, 'Temenia' and 'Sougia' to the right, as is Saint Anna. We also turn right and follow the rising road basically ENE, overall, to the tall olives and tidy houses of signposted Koufalotos, a pleasing village strung out alongside the ascending road that swings left, i.e. N. At this point look out for a water well by an impressive platania (plane tree).

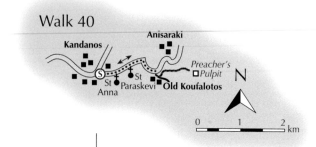

Walk 40

Anisaraki
Kandanos
Preacher's
Pulpit
St
St Paraskevi Old Koufalotos
Anna

N

0 1 2 km

By tree (2) and well leave the tarmac road right for a concrete pathway that gradually ascends through Old Koufalotos. Today it is a series of crumbling, abandoned village houses, although at the far end several are well tended and occupied. Walk E, and as you pass by white-walled Number 12, swing left on a stony donkey track that rises for a short distance onto a distinct stone and dirt E–W track. Take the W way, admiring the landscapes of the saucered plateau carpeted with grove upon grove of thriving silver-green olives, in the centre of which sits Kandanos.

After 100m on this zigzag way we meet a further track descending on the right. Join this track, i.e. turn right onto another scenic zigzag. We are now walking N; to the right above note the overhang of protruding rock crowned by a single rounded olive tree. At the next angled bend on the right we have a choice of a sharp ascent to the rock and single tree, or carrying on ahead. 10 paces from the last bend take a thin path – stepped – through the ground-hugging scrub with the slabbed outcrop of naked rock and 'umbrella' tree directly above. Pass through a gate in the wire fence for the final metres on a thin trod E, through stone and scrub, to 'Preacher's Pulpit' (3).

From this fine balcony at 750m (2460ft) there are stunning views to the west of Kandanos and its fertile surrounds, encircled by mountain and ridge. Descend, initially with care, on the paths and tracks of ascent to the old village of Koufalotos. At the white walls of Number 12 turn right, i.e. W, through the old houses to emerge onto the road by the well and platania. Swing left, descending overall SW, into Kandanos at its eastern end. Note as the houses are reached on the eastern fringe of the town the broken remains of Byzantine Saint Paraskevi.

Items of Interest

(1) **KANDANOS**. Kandanos (modern spelling – Kantanos is the old spelling) is a proud town that rose from the ashes of old Kantanos after the holocaust of 1945. It is remembered with dignity on 6 June by representatives of the Allied forces involved in the 1941–45 conflict. On that day, in June 2004, I was on the heights south of Kandanos and Vamvakades (pronounced 'Bambakades') quietly listening to the moving, musical tributes of the national anthems of Greece, Britain and France, in commemoration of the fallen. Memories in this capital of Selinos are long and sad – even today you will not find a single postcard for sale.

(2) **TREES**. Trees flourish on this mountain- and ridge-ringed plateau of Kandanos, from olives, the 'divine' or 'golden' tree of the Ancient Greeks, to the stately groves of castanea (sweet chestnut), figs and pencil-thin cypresses. So prolific do they grow and prosper that the entire plateau appears, from mountain and ridge top, to be awash with varying shades of green.

(3) **PREACHER'S PULPIT**. This rock, positioned due east from the centre of Kandanos, is so-named after a resident of these parts who was of a mind to spread the word from this outcrop to an imaginary congregation far below in and around Kandanos.

WALK 41

In Search of Byzantine Art

Saint Nicholas, Saint Mamas, Panagia, Saint Iannis, Prophet Elias, Saint Catherine, Kandanos Cathedral

Distance	12km (7½ miles)
Height Gain	150m (492ft)
Start/Finish	Kandanos
Grade	3
Walking Time	4–4½ hours
Maps	EFSTATHIADIS 1:79,000 CHANIA ISBN 960 226 531 0
	harms IC verlag 1:100,000 Western Crete
	ISBN 3–927468–16–9
Accommodation	Kandanos (limited) plus refreshments

Charismatic, rewarding, photogenic, historic, unique and scenically pleasing – all are applicable to this physically easy, mentally stimulating walk through centuries of Selinos' Byzantine culture.

The Route

From central Kandanos (1), above Saint Nicholas (2), walk N via the main street to a junction, signed 'Chania' half-left and 'Sougia' right. At this junction walk left past a 'Silk' petrol station and immediately turn left onto a tarmacked lane signposted 'Saint Mamas' in the district of Lofos, our second port of call 1km (²/₃ mile) N from Kandanos. The quiet lane, N and W, is an arborial delight, with silvery olives, bright green *moura* and shimmering eucalyptus. At the T-junction, left Saint Mamas, right Hatsoudiana (our return route), turn left to meet ahead Saint Mamas (3), surrounded by marble graves.

Continue in a westerly direction past houses, occupied and unoccupied, swinging half-left and right with deteriorating buildings, right. Descend W to the last dilapidated farm building onto the narrow, initially overgrown donkey track between fences descending W, past right-hand broken walls, then S through olives, into a clearing lined with chestnut (identified by ribbed bark and serrated green leaves). Ahead, alongside our track, stands the simple Church of Saint Panagia (4) with red pantiles and external bell tower.

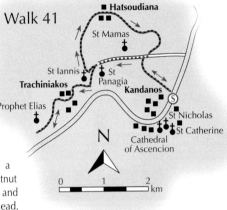

Walk 41

- **Hatsoudiana**
- St Mamas ✝
- St Iannis ✝ / St Panagia ✝
- **Trachiniakos**
- Prophet Elias ✝
- **Kandanos**
- S
- St Nicholas ✝
- St Catherine ✝
- Cathedral of Ascencion

N

0   1   2 km

Continue W and SW through continuing olives on a widening, stone-lined track approaching a bamboo-lined watercourse (dry in summer). At a junction of streams

Virgin Mary (Panagia), Skoudiana

Prophet Elias,
Trachiniakos

cross the right-hand one to ascend the steps onto the roadway. Standing on the bridge, note left 100m SE a T-junction connecting the Kandanos–Paleochora highway. Right, i.e. W, signed 'Saint Iannis' (5), our fourth church, 150m distant by the roadside, its conifer-shaded pillared bell tower 9m from the church door. Surrounding the church are marble graves, inside are wall paintings to excite.

Should time be at a premium, this absorbing walk can be reduced after inspecting Saint Iannis. Return to Kandanos from Saint Iannis as per the outward route instructions in reverse, saving the journey to Prophet Elias for another day, or Walk 45.

Continue W from Saint Iannis for 1km (²⁄₃ mile) on an olive-lined tarmac lane, site of contorted olives and climbing, scavenging goats, to the scattered village of Trachiniakos. Follow the main road descending right and then left to cross the second bridge over the Kakodikianos river. Once over, turn left at a garage (private), walking alongside the watercourse for ½km to a manmade concrete water retainer. To the right a concrete road climbs steeply to Prophet Elias church (6), crowned with chamfered bell tower and red pantiles, classic Byzantine that demands inspection.

Return to Saint Iannis and the bridge. ◀

Continue with the ascending zigzag roadway, passing old and renovated houses, through tree-clad hillsides (laid bare by severe landslips). Beyond, on the right, are the remains of an old farm and olive press – **only look, the buildings are insecure**. Continue via a donkey track parallel with the road, N and NNE. Rejoin the road for a pleasing mix of road and donkey track walking through tidy, prosperous, half-hidden tree-shaded farms.

Beyond Hatsoudiana take the donkey track left, between wall and fence, as far as a junction. Turn right (one side wired and walled) through olives, emerging onto the road between two houses, where a colourful bush illuminates the fence. On the road pass over what is in May a dry riverbed, walking mainly S, by a right-hand zigzag, to a shaded section of platania, rounding a corner to the T-junction (signed 'Saint Mamas') met on our outward journey.

Return to Kandanos for the final church, Saint Catherine (7). From the 'Silk' petrol station cross the road to the 'Sougia' signposted road E, ascending to meet an immediate incoming road from the right – identified by the ruin of Saint Paraskevi. Turn right, walking towards the twin-towered Cathedral of the Ascencion. At the end of the road turn left for 50m to externally restored Saint Catherine, crouching left, the final Byzantine church of this ecclesiastic exploration.

Items of Interest

(1) **KANDANOS**. Ancient Kantanos, or Kandania, 'The City of Victory' began during Roman occupation around 69BC, under Cointo Caecilio Metello, lasting until the middle of the fourth century. Byzantine Kandanos was succeeded by the Venetian occupation of 1212, followed by the Turkish occupation of 1645–1897.

(2) **SAINT NICHOLAS**. Adjacent to the cathedral, Saint Nicholas operated as the city cathedral after the devastation of the Second World War, until the Cathedral of the Ascencion was completed. During Turkish occupation, 1645–1913, it was used as a mosque. It wasn't until centuries later that its plaster overlay was discovered to have hidden Byzantine paintings beneath, together with marble from much older Christian buildings.

223

(3) **SAINT MAMAS**. In the district of Lofos north of Kandanos, Saint Mamas' wall paintings date from 1355–56, including *The Crucifixion of Christ* and *The Ascension*.

(4) **PANAGIA**. Panagia (Virgin Mary) is northwest of Kandanos in Skoudiana district, its bell suspended between two external columns. Surrounding the building are church stones from the fifth and sixth centuries, confirming the presence of early Christian buildings, as do broken marble columns. Note wall paintings: *Dormition of Virgin Mary*, *Virgin Mary*, *The Platytera* and *Baptism of Christ*.

(5) **SAINT IANNIS**. Saint Iannis is also known as St John the Forerunner. The church has a detached two-tiered bell tower (9m from the church). Walls painted 1328–29 are in good condition. Note *St Prokopios* and *Archangel Gabriel*. Building materials display presence of pre-Christian building.

(6) **PROPHET ELIAS**. Majority of wall paintings are in good condition, particularly a bearded Christ and *The Prophet Elias*. The base of the altar is decorated by 'the presentation of a bird', thought to be an old Christian shield of arms, also found in goldleaf above the main door of the main church, Panagia, in Vlatos (Walk 26).

(7) **SAINT CATHERINE**. A recent exterior restoration. Only two clear paintings survive – a frieze of decorative tiles and *The Donor's Inscription*.

(8) **CATHEDRAL OF THE ASCENCION**. Twin-towered, the cathedral stands proud above the central square of Kandanos, alongside the municipal offices of Selinos. Construction of this charismatic building had hardly begun when, in June 1941, for 10 days, the German army reduced Kandanos to rubble. This crime against humanity is recorded on a marble plaque below the cathedral at the perimeter of the town's Remembrance Square. 'Here stood Kandanos. It was destroyed in revenge for the murder of 25 German soldiers.'

WALK 42

High Above Kandanos

Kandanos, Saint Kyriaki Route, Saint Giorgios, Vamvakades, Koufalotos Church, Kandanos

Distance	14.5km (9 miles)
Height Gain	500m (1641ft)
Start/Finish	Kandanos
Grade	3–4
Walking Time	6 hours
Maps	EFSTATHIADIS 1:79,000 CHANIA ISBN 960 226 531 0
	harms IC verlag 1:100,000 Western Crete (includes E4)
	ISBN 3–927468–16–9
Accommodation	Kandanos – apartments (limited); refreshments

A varied, challenging walk, south and east of Kandanos, that scales the high ridges overlooking the olive-clad plateau cradling charismatic Kandanos. A delight in May, when deciduous leaves are green and the air is full of scents and singing birds.

The Route

From the roadside chapel of Saint Catherine, walk S through an avenue of olives, waymarked with a yellow arrowhead → 'Saint Kyriaki', via tarmac lanes, donkey tracks and stone and dirt tracks to pass, left, House Number 125. At the next U-bend in the lane, take the stone-stepped, narrow donkey track left, cutting out two legs on the lane.

Rejoin the tarmac, veer right and continue past scented roses and silver-green olives. Cross a bridge over a stream, flanked by colourful broadleaves, including walnuts, to pass farm buildings and a house W, before a waymarked fork in the track. The sign → is right to Saint

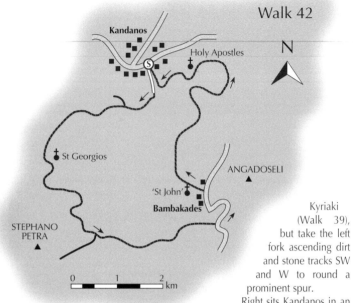

Walk 42

Kandanos

Holy Apostles

N

† St Georgios

'St John' †
ANGADOSELI ▲

Bambakades

STEPHANO
PETRA ▲

0   1   2 km

Kyriaki
(Walk 39),
but take the left
fork ascending dirt
and stone tracks SW
and W to round a
prominent spur.

Right sits Kandanos in an
olive-clad basin. Continue
ascending, N of W, to reveal rounded
summits and jutting spurs on the southern summit ridge.
At the final corner (Kandanos now unseen) we have our
first sighting of an interesting rocky outcrop rising due S
– more of that later!

Continue ascending to meet Byzantine Saint
Georgios and its freestanding bell. Should you enter the
church **beware the low lintel above the church door**.
The area around is known as 'Three Churches' (1). 100m
beyond Saint Georgios are the remains of two more,
although I only saw the remains of one, beneath trackside scrub. From Saint Georgios ascend S, past a
vineyard, with many villages now visible N, as we
approach our 'rocky outcrop goal', rising right and round
the next spur. In May the surrounds are colourful –
flowers abound and birds are in full voice and full flight.

Swing right, i.e. W then WNW, at the head of a narrow, chestnut-, fig- and plane-tree-filled gully. Several hundred metres above the olive groves we arrive at a T-junction. The right hand is gated, the left one marks the path taking us NE on a 'fire-ravaged' hillside towards the summit ridge crowned by rocky outcrops. Continue ascending, and as we pass between two trees, Vamvakades (pronounced 'Bambakades') to the east comes into view. Meet and cross a busy stream, cloaked by giant, very green broadleaved trees – a mini jungle.

The track forks right, i.e. due S, rising beneath giant oak. Beyond, pass through a wiremesh gate to ascend left, via a track, initially E and S, onto an overgrown pathway. The curving track ascends, left and left again, i.e. E. At the T-junction ahead fork left, E, leading to a sharper curving ascent, E, then S, then W, for the final metres to the prominent rocky outcrops (2), favoured by local goats. The final zigzags present no problems. Beyond the largest outcrop a slightly lower 'cubic stone' resembling a stovepipe hat catches the eye. Leave the outcrop and zigzag to the top of the summit ridge – note a roadside abandoned tractor and Bambakades, below conical Angadoseli, to the east.

Walk S then E, i.e. left, amid a maze of visible dirt tracks, towards two communication masts ahead, to pass through a well-secured wiremesh gate, left, onto a rising concrete lane. On this stretch, S, the shimmering Libyan Sea is visible below Anidri and beyond Akrotiri Flomos. Travelling E skirt above a deep gully, left, to meet the tarmacked Bambakades–Temenia road. Turn left, walking N for approximately 70m to a bend left heading a series of descending tree-lined zigzags to the six road-side houses of Bambakades. At its northern end turn sharp left, descending by concrete lane to the modernised church. (I have drawn a blank regarding its name – its predecessor was St John).

Pass right of the church, descending NW via a gated, oak-lined, rapidly descending track with a sharp drop right. It's a winding descent with unmarked forks, but no problem if you continue on the main (wider and worn)

Kandanos to east ridge and Stephano Petra

track winding NW, through an outstanding collection of broadleaves. Old Koufalotos can be seen ahead and below. Fork left to the octagonal, pantiled Church of Koufalotos (The Holy Apostles) (3). Pass on a concrete track leading to a group of white houses. Walk through on a narrow road rising beyond the last, large house on the right. A few metres beyond, swing right onto a dirt and stone track through descending olive groves, which becomes, at a T-junction, a donkey track. Follow this short track left to the Kandanos–Saint Kyriaki road, close to rose-clad House Number 125.

Turn right for the final few hundred metres into the street of Saint Catherine and the centre of Kandanos.

Items of Interest
(1) **THE THREE CHURCHES**. Only one remains, Saint Georgios. A second lies broken, half–hidden 100m

beyond the restored Saint Georgios, 2002, verified on its freestanding bell. Within Saint Georgios the best wall paintings are on the north (left) side of the interior. Writing appears on both sides.

(2) **ROCKY OUTCROPS**. These are prominent on a jutting shoulder high above the olive-green saucer cradling Kandanos. They could be sandstone, and the geometrical slabs and blocks are a favourite resting place for local goats. They are also one half of two compass points – the other is Kandanos Cathedral – that have given me, in all my years of hillwalking in wild and lonely places, my one and only exact compass bearing, registering a perfect S to N. To verify, the reading was checked in reverse, from cathedral N to S to the visible outcrop on the ridge, resulting in an identical 180° reading.

(3) **KOUFALOTOS CHURCH**. The Holy Apostles has no church bell. In the Second World War the church doubled up as a centre of resistance, utilising the one post office telephone in Kandanos. The missing church bell is said to lie under the sod of a nearby field. Wall paintings within the church are coated with deposits of salt, leaving only five that can be recognised.

WALK 43

To Elusive Spina and Beyond

Saint Antonios, Spinatiko, Spina Village, Saint Zinon, Below Vigla and Apopigadi

Distance	18.5km (11½ miles)
Height Gain	900m (2953ft)
Start/Finish:	Saint Antonios
Grade	3, in places 4, depending on start/finish point
Walking Time	7–8 hours
Maps	EFSTATHIADIS 1:79,000 CHANIA ISBN 960 226 5310
	harms IC verlag 1:100,000 Western Crete (includes E4)
	ISBN 3-927468-16-9

Accommodation Kandanos – apartments (limited) and refreshments

From Saint Antonios to Spina, and above to the heights of Strogili Korofi – domed/rounded hill – and Vigla 1234m (4049ft) is, if you are contemplating the entire journey there and back on foot, a long and serious undertaking. Varying views, however, reward the walker. Start from Saint Antonios, a halfway house that can be reached by taxi/car, via twisting stony tracks, leaving the quarry roads behind in favour of pathways through 'Spinatiko' (1) gorge to Spina and beyond. I was fortunate to get a lift to the church, although my return from Saint Zinon to Kandanos was entirely by foot.

The Route

Saint Antonios is reached (by car or on foot) from Kandanos. From the main street go NE on the Chania road for 1¼km (¾ mile), passing the school, to a sharp left-hand bend in the road. At this junction, marked by two statues, the Spina road veers right, i.e. E, then N for a monotonous zigzag on wide tarmac and dirt and

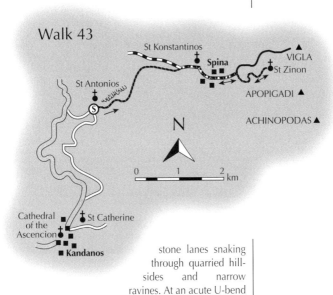

stone lanes snaking through quarried hillsides and narrow ravines. At an acute U-bend in the valley floor, 3.5km (2¼ miles) from the junction above Kandanos, stand the pristine white walls and ten tiny windows of the church of Saint Antonios (2). Not so appealing are the nearby goat pens! From here the walk begins.

Walk E from the church via a tree-sheltered dirt track, crossing a bridge over a dry watercourse into a narrowing gorge. The only minus preventing perfection is the increasing numbers of loose stones underfoot – care is required. A 'musical gorge' of constant birdsong and tinkling goat bells, sage and rock abound, contorted trees provide shade, and after 15 minutes into the gorge we meet a crosstracks.

Take the most narrow defile left, i.e. N (with electric poles and track), although initially it appears too narrow for comfort. It is intriguing and never claustrophobic, this northern narrow passageway into which the sun never shines. Release, as the walls widen, is gradual as we

The narrow mouth of Spina Gorge

ascend to cross a dry, wandering watercourse several times. Ascent is now steady, with the sun filtering through the canopy of castanea and platania. Coned rocky outcrops and small hillocks rise ahead as the gorge widens and we ascend 20° E of N through this lonely, scenic ravine. Now walking N, 700–750m (2297–2461ft) above sea level, cross the streambed again, making for the conspicuous, conical rocky outcrop ahead, gaining height. On the right, clinging to the watercourse, is a line of bright-green castanea, ahead a towering mountain ridge 1200m (3937ft) dominates the eastern horizons above Kandanos.

At the tree-clad coned outcrop (two more round the corner), break out of the ravine floor, turn right and rise onto a farm track. **Care is needed on the initial sections as landslips have eaten into the water-eroded dirt and stone way.** Our rocky surrounds are scenically pleasing, but also a bit of a suntrap, as we make a U-turn at the head of the gorge, swinging right over a concrete ford and rising into the extensive fertile basin that lies below the western flanks of mount Vigla – 'Twin Peaks'.

In this 'Garden of Eden' Spina nestles. Our track gradually ascends S and SW, rounding many olive-clad shoulders. Pause awhile to look back into the gorge to see how narrow its eastern portals are before continuing N and E towards the peaks of Vigla. Spina and its churches remain hidden as our track links with a wide tarmac road, swinging right to reveal Spina's roofs and corners, below right and above left, as the route twists along the olive-shaded lane.

Some houses appear abandoned – note the laneside café–bar (closed whenever I have passed). Beyond, the road forks right beneath ancient chestnuts, taking us beyond the village, via dirt roads, S and SE, through groves of giant oak. Apopigadi, in addition to Vigla and Strogili Korifi, provides a dramatic canvas, framed by bright-green acres of venerable castanea, of the peaks and rock-strewn ridges.

Vigla, NE from Spina, shelters on the 1200m (3937ft) contour the born-again Church of Saint Zinon (2). Continue NE, ascending steadily on the goat-occupied stony track to a prominent T-junction. Take the sharp-right route ascending and winding to the base of the conical rock sheltering the to-be-restored Church of Saint Zinon (2). The conical rock I have called 'Zinon Rock', a distinct landmark of this green-and-grey highland patchwork. From this secluded rock return to Spina via the outward track.

From the community of Spina descend via the confines of the gorge of ascent to Saint Antonios. If you don't have pre-arranged transport it's a 3 hour hike downhill, passing giant quarries, a football pitch and the senior school, back to Kandanos.

ITEMS OF INTEREST

(1) **SPINATIKO**. The Spina Gorge is a main gorge with offshoots that runs northeast and east to the village of Spina. This *farangi* ('gorge' or 'gully') has as its entrance the white-walled church of Saint Anthony. Although narrow and barren in places, the gorge provides homes and food for a range of birds, in the region of 26 nesting species, including large raptors, e.g. eagles and vultures, and mammals, plus a variety of trees and colourful, ground-hugging plants.

Saint Zinon by 'Zinon Rock'

(2) **SPINA'S CHURCHES**. Below Spinatiko stands the picturesque church of Saint Antonios, with no surviving wall paintings. An engraved dove perches on the apex of its eastern roof. Within tree-hidden Spina there stands Saint ΕΙΡΗΝΑΙΟΣ (Eftihia), dedicated to Panagia (the Virgin Mary). The wall paintings in this Byzantine church have faded through the centuries. There is also Saint Konstantinos, above a roadside spring with a metal drinking cup, and a telegraph pole at the west end. The most interesting is Saint Zinon (*zinios* means wind), which in earlier years stood high on the wind- and storm-lashed slopes of Vigla, and required repeated restoration. However, a saviour, a man from Spina who emigrated to America and prospered, remembered the storm-battered church. He made financial arrangements through his niece, Soula Mathewdaki, for a church to be built on the leeside of the conical rock, ensuring the family will indeed receive their 'favour' (*kati kalo* – 'good for you') when it is completed.

WALK 44

*Kandanos' Old Ways to
and from Anisaraki*

Kandanos, Old Koufalotos, Anisaraki,
'Ancient Olive Wood', Donkey Trail
and Church Routes, Kandanos

Distance	5–6km (3¾ miles)
Height Gain	150m (492ft)
Start/Finish	Kandanos
Grade	1–2
Walking Time	2–3 hours
Maps	EFSTATHIADIS 1:79,000 CHANIA (with footpaths)
	ISBN 960 226 531 0
	harms IC verlag 1:100,000 Western Crete (includes E4)
	ISBN 3-927468-16-9
Accommodation	Kandanos – apartments (limited), refreshments

This leisurely circular walk along the old ways begins at the restored church of Saint Catherine, below and east of the Cathedral of the Ascension. Underfoot a variety of tarmac lanes, dirt and stone tracks, old donkey trails, church routes and flower- and olive-lined pathways north-east to Anisaraki. From Anisaraki we follow a descending donkey trail/church route return to Kandanos.

The Route

With Saint Catherine's on your left walk S, passing several new houses, through an avenue of olives with mountains and ridges ahead. This first section, waymarked in places with a yellow arrowhead → 'Saint Kyriaki', takes us via tarmac lanes to join old donkey tracks between olive groves, sweet chestnut and giant platania. Initially go with the waymarks to pass on your

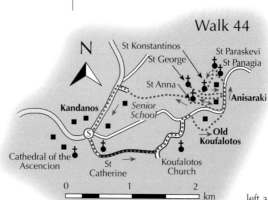

Walk 44

St Konstantinos
St George
St Paraskevi
St Panagia
St Anna
Anisaraki
Kandanos
Senior School
Old Koufalotos
Cathedral of the
Ascencion
St Catherine
Koufalotos Church

0   1   2
km

left a flower-clad house, Number 125. 30m or so beyond, at a right-angle bend in the lane, leave left with the narrow, ascending, stone-stepped donkey track (cutting out a lengthy U-bend on the tarmac lane). When the tarmac is met again, at another U-bend, carry on with the donkey track half-left and ahead, ascending through olive groves to a large roadside house. Turn left onto the road, following it NE past several houses.

Beyond the white-walled houses a concrete track leads to the octagonal, pantiled Church of Koufalotos (1). The route continues past a dairy and goat pens to veer left onto the main road leading to Anisaraki. Turn right for a short ascent on the tarmac road to meet a giant platania and a well on the right. Turn right at the well to the aged village of Old Koufalotos. At the white house – Number 12 – turn sharp left on an ascending stony path, past yapping dogs, to a dirt and stone track. Turn left, i.e. W, and follow this twisting, descending scenic track – beware mating snakes up to a metre in length – to rejoin the quiet, tarmacked Anisaraki road. Veer right and continue on the road for a short distance to a 'shot-up' signpost announcing 'Anisaraki', and close by a post listed 'Saint Anna' (2) (we return later to this point).

Carry on with the twisting road half-right through the village as the road winds, swinging to our right and ignoring small side roads. At a makeshift building on a bend swing left, as directed by the straightening road and the signpost on the left, rising on a concrete and stone/dirt track to the churches of Saint Panagia and Saint Paraskevi (2). Ascend the short distance to the attractive fenced church of Saint Panagia (locked), with its separate four-pillars bell tower, before and below the older, smaller second church, Saint Paraskevi (unlocked).

Leave the churches by turning right from the lower church down a donkey track N, between olive and fig, winding left onto a tarmac road to meet another of Anisaraki's churches, Saint Konstantinos, the church of Anisaraki's tidy cemetery of marble graves. This church, Number 29, has a bell tower and shelter on the opposite side of the road and contains churchwarden-style upright seats.

Return from this church S, and at the first fork swing right with the tarmac road, descending W through olive groves to join the main road. Turn right to descend due W initially, then S, a pleasing walk lined with thriving trees. A derelict house on the left (Number 38) is passed

The church and cemetery of Saint Konstantinos, Anisaraki

Saint George, Anisaraki

as we approach a sign, 'Saint George', on the right. As directed, turn right, passing houses, mainly on the left, to continue on the winding, overall N track to reach a fenced Y-junction. Take the right-hand fork (a small piece of metal on a fencepost shows a blue symbol of a church cross and an arrow to the right). 100m on the right the small Church of Saint George stands, with red pantiles, white walls and locked door.

Return to the directional marker (blue) to veer left, continuing on the stone and dirt track to the main road E of S, finally met beyond a collection of ageing agricultural machinery. Turn right, ie. SW, to meet signposted

Saint Anna, turning right, i.e. W, onto a descending lane to the tiny church a few metres to the right. After inspection ensure you close the door and the gate with the tiny bolt on the top left, and also the wire-fence gate leading onto the track.

Turn right onto the olive-tree-shaded concrete track, initially between stone wall and wire fence, a pleasing descending way approximately W. At the first crossroads cross over and continue descending on a line towards the now visible towers of the Cathedral of Kandanos to reach and pass the senior school buildings. Turn left onto the main Chania road, passing the olive press and the 'Silk' petrol station to return to Kandanos.

Items of Interest

(1) **KOUFALOTOS CHURCH**. Koufalotos church, The Holy Apostles, has no church bell. In the Second World War the church doubled up as a centre of resistance, utilising the one post office telephone in Kandanos. The missing church bell is said to lie under the sod of a nearby field. The wall paintings within the church are coated with deposits of salt, leaving only five that can be recognised.

(2) **ANISARAKI CHURCHES**. Saint Panagia contains several recognisable wall paintings (painted 14th–15th century). The sharpest in outline is perhaps *The Descent to Hades* and certainly the most interesting and thought provoking is *The Sea Giving up the Dead*, where the most dominant feature is *Woman Riding a Beast*.

Saint Paraskevi stands a few metres from Saint Panagia, and sadly its paintings are faded. Saint George is watched over by cypress trees. Its internal wall paintings were 'drawn over' in 1917, according to K. Lassithiotakis, author of Churches of Western Crete, 'by a completely ignorant painter'.

Saint Anna is said to have 'many remarkable wall paintings' from 1457–62, the most outstanding thought to be *Saint Anna Breastfeeding the Virgin Mary*.

WALK 45

Kandanos to Plemeniana:

An Ancient Trail

Kandanos, Trachiniakos, Plemeniana

Distance	4km (2½ miles)
Height loss	Zero
Start/Finish	Kandanos/Plemeniana
Grade	2
Walking Time	1½ hours
Maps	EFSTATHIADIS 1:79,000 CHANIA ISBN 960 226 531 0
	harms IC verlag 1:100,000 Western Crete (includes E4)
	ISBN 3-927468-16-9
Accommodation	Kandanos – Hotel Apopigadi, apartments (limited)

A delightful valley-floor walk close to the tinkling waters of the Kakodikian River. Full of birdsong, it winds through olive groves, fruit orchards and small villages, passing Byzantine churches of great interest.

An ancient donkey trail/church route/commercial artery alongside and above the River Kakodikianos journeyed southwest and south from the city of Kandanos to the Libyan Sea at Paleochora. At the time of research plans are in hand to resurrect, waymark and reopen this ancient trail, so that academics and lovers of the great outdoors can study and appreciate the Cretan country-side and the ways of their forebears in centuries past.

The route is to be cleaned, waymarked – a gold cross on a red background – stepped and fenced, walls rein-forced, rest and picnic areas provided, springs cleansed and tapped, with occasional WCs along the way. It

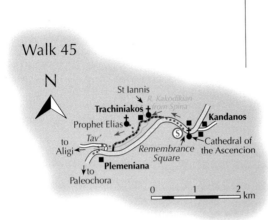

Walk 45

N

St Iannis

Trachiniakos

R. Kakodikian from Spina

Kandanos

Prophet Elias

Tav'

to Aligi

Remembrance Square

Cathedral of the Ascencion

Plemeniana

↓to Paleochora

0   1   2 km

passes through or fringes the settlements of Trachiniakos, Plemeniana, Kakodiki (Machia), Vlithias, Kalamos, and Spaniakos (5) in the Kakodikian river valley to Paleochora. Also met en route will be information boards. Historic and traditional structures encountered are Byzantine churches, water mills, stone springs, wells, stone benches, and a classic stone packhorse (humpbacked) bridge at Kakodiki (Machia) (seen also in Sirikari Gorge (Walk 17)).

From Kandanos the route can be divided into two sections, first beyond Trachiniakos passing several fine Byzantine churches to Plemeniana. This section is described here, and although not waymarked, is on good tracks and country roads, and can be walked with ease, comfort and interest.

The second section is south from Plemeniana to Paleochora. At the time of writing path clearance and route preparation has not begun due to funds being diverted to priorities such as road repairs and reconstruction, bridge building, and water and electricity supplies for outlying villages. In the meantime the scrub continues to strangle the proposed route.

The Route

Begin the walk at the foot of Kandanos Cathedral, by Remembrance Square, walking alongside the main road to Paleochora for a short distance to the sign 'Health Centre of Kandanos' (1). A minor road forks and descends right to the tree-clad valley floor, indicating this is the route to the church of Saint Ioannis (Saint John the Forerunner) (2). As the valley floor is reached, ignore the roadway crossing the bridge right (Walk 41). Carry on NNW straight ahead to the signposted, now visible, Church of Saint Ioannis, with its independent two-tier bell tower. To pass by this small, simple but charismatic Byzantine church would be to ignore the heart and soul of the entire walk, such is the excellence of the enthralling display of Byzantine art gracing the walls and ceiling within.

From Saint Ioannis continue W for 1km (⅔ mile) to the fertile surrounds of the scattered village of Trachiniakos, passing a grove of 'corkscrew olives' and a line of productive oranges on the right, and a new, heavily gated mansion house on the left, before crossing a central bridge over the Kakodikianos river – from Spina – then a smaller one. Swing left past a private garage and commence one of the most pleasing and fertile stretches of the walk, with the now hidden river always audible. Half a kilometre or so ahead stands a trackside concrete water tank, on the right, beside a rapidly rising concrete track to the ecclesiastical jewel of the Church of Prophet Elias (3). It also is worth a visit.

Remembrance Square, Kandanos

*Semi-tropical
Plemeniana*

Return to the trackside water tank, turn right and continue with the broad track, beneath venerable olives, to initially fluctuate between SW and W, twisting at times towards S, as the way gently rises and falls. This is an ideal route that even in the height of summer is comfortable to walk. Ignore tracks and lanes leading up to the right. As the surface changes to concrete and ascends, continue W between shady castanea and olive, and at the Y-junction take the left fork, ablaze with flowers in May, while on the ridge ahead two red-and-white communications masts spear skywards. The rising track on the right is ignored – stay on the one veering left, overall S, descending on a sweeping curve. A tidy, flower-laden house, surrounded by a low, white-painted wall is passed to join the Aligi–Plemeniana road.

Turn right just beyond a joinery business onto the Aligi road for 200m. O Mylos Taverna (4) can be seen ahead on the right. Before the highly recommended taverna, turn left to cross a bridge and rise on a dirt and stone path through gardens to the main Kandanos–Paleochora road that runs through thè settlement of Plemeniana, a drawn-out roadside village of giant cactus and many flowers.

Until such time as the Plemeniana to Paleochora section is completed, a return to Kandanos is recommended either by the outward route on foot or by the Paleochora–Kandanos service bus (4 per day).

243

ITEMS OF INTEREST

(1) **KANDANOS**. Its history dates back thousands of years, into ancient times. Kandania, as it was known, means 'City of Victory'. At the beginning of the Roman Period, beginning 69BC, it was overseen by Cointus Caecillius Metellus. The Roman Period lasted until the middle of the fourth century, to be followed by the Byzantine Period, which lasted to the early years of the 13th century, to be displaced by Venetian conquerors in 1212. They in turn relinquished rule to the Ottoman Turks, who from 1645 to 1897–1913 attempted to replace Greek Christian Orthodoxy with Islam. They failed thanks to the indomitable spirit of the Cretan race.

(2) and (3) **BYZANTINE CHURCHES**. Saint Ioannis and Prophet Elias. At the beginning of the 20th century there were approximately 130 churches from the 13th to 16th centuries. Today approximately 19 survive within the structural and artistic category of 'Good' or 'Very Good', with clear, restored wall paintings. Five or so remain semi-ruins, while others are recent replacements of complete ruins. Examples of all categories can be seen on many of the Selinos walks, in particular this walk and Walk 41, 'In Search of Byzantine Art'.

(4) The roadside watercourse alongside the O Mylos Taverna is much favoured by families of black, 2ft long eels (*geli*, pronounced 'killy'). They also like the taverna's food.

(5) **VILLAGES EN ROUTE**. These suffered a great deal during the 1645–1913 Turkish occupation of Crete. Many were occupied by Turkish families, Spaniakos in particular, where Cretan families were forced to convert to Islam. Towers were built on the heights above to provide signalling facilities between villages – note the Tower of Kantanoli in Vlithias. In 1670 the entire population of Spaniakos was forced to adopt the Islamic faith, and the largest mosque in all of Crete was built in the village. Today the village school stands on the site.

APPENDIX 1
Glossary of Names and Local Terms

Kreta	Kriti/Crete
Anglia	England
Scotia	Scotland
O ha'rtis	The map
Nisi	Island
Akrotiri	Cape
Thalasa	Sea
Kolpos Kissamou	Gulf of Kissamos
Liviko Pelagos	Libyan Sea
Ormos Selino Kastelli	Bay of Castle of Selinos
Plaz	Beach
Potami	River
Nero	Water
Neraki	Drinking water
Vrisi	Spring/water-tap
Keros	Weather (*kalos keros* – good weather)
Ilyos	Sun
Aeras	Wind
Iremi/bonatza	Calm
Hynoi	Snow
Poli	City/town
Hotel	Hotel
Domatia	Rooms
Poso kano?	How much?
Banio	Bath
Doos	Shower
Taverna	Restaurant
Krasi	Wine (*aspro* – white, *kokino* – red)
Bira	Beer
Potiri	Glass
To Faghito	The meal
Psari	Fish
Kotopoolo	Chicken
Keftethes	Meat-balls
Psomi	Bread
Tiri	Cheese
cafenion	Cafe (*kafe* – coffee, *tsai* – tea, *zahari* – sugar, *ghala* – milk)
Parakalo	Please
Megalo	Large (*micro* – small)
Polee	Much/many
Zeste	Hot
Creo	Cold
Lego	Little/small
Poo ine	Where is
Kendro	Town centre
Platiea	Town Square
Hora	Village
Voono	Mountain
Fotoghrafiki mihani	Camera
Monopatti	Footpath
Kalderimi	Stone-slabbed donkey track
Yeffy-rah	Bridge
Spilari (also known as *koumi* and *mitato*)	Stone shelter/ shepherd's mountain hut
Aloni	A stone circle in which ripe grain is winnowed
Fili moo	My friend
Aftaa	That's it!
Epharistó	Thank you

APPENDIX 2
Further Reading

Quick and Easy Greek, Teach Yourself, Hodder and Stoughton, 1994
   ISBN 0 340 38766 1

Crete – The Traveller's Guide, Eberhard Fohrer, Springfield Books Ltd, 1990
   ISBN 0-947655–86–7

Crete – The White Mountains, Lorraine Wilson, Cicerone Press, 2000,
   reprinted 2002, ISBN 1 85284 298 9

Kissamos – Green Tourism Guide of Kissamos Province (Kissamos Tourist Offices)
   Includes walks, history, churches, folklore, flora and fauna, and accommodation

Blue Guide Crete, Pat Cameron, 7th edition, WW Norton, ISBN 0 3933 2134 7

Municipality of Inahorion – 'Our Place1/4Our Living', a local tourism leaflet guide

Zorba the Greek, Nikos Kazantzakis, Faber and Faber ISBN 0 6848 2554 6

Paleochora (A Look Back into the Past), Nicolaos Pyrovolakis, (printer Mich.
   Georvassakis), 1998. Relates to Paleochora walks and walks in and around
   Kandanos

The Byzantine Churches of Kandanos, The Cultural Association 'Kandania', 1999
   ISBN 960–86475–0–9 Highly recommended

Birds and Mammals of Crete, George Sfikas, Efstathiades Group, 1987

Also *Trees and Shrubs of Greece*, 1979; *Wild Flowers of Crete*, 1978

The Cretan Runner, George Psychoundakis (trans. PL Fermor), Penguin
   ISBN 0 1402 7322 0

The Fall of Crete, Alan Clark, Cassell ISBN 0 3043 5348 5

Ten Days to Destiny, GC Kiriakopoulos, Holy Cross Orthodox Press
   ISBN 0 9176 5349 1

APPENDIX 3
Useful Information

Name of Service	Telephone Code	Number
CHANIA		
Medical Emergency		166
Police, Flying Squad		100
Fire Department		199
Bus Station	0821	93052
Airport, Arrivals and Departures	0821	63264
KISSAMOS		
Medical Centre	0822	22222
Regional Centres -		
Kaludiana	0822	31484
Kalathena	0822	51249
Platanos	0822	41227
Elos	0822	61227
Kefali	0822	61333
Kolimbari	0824	22204
Police		
Kissamos Department	0822	22115
Gramvousa Department	0822	41203
Dept of Kolymbari	0824	22100
Dept of Drapania	0822	41203
Dept of Topolia	0822	51210
Dept of Elos	0822	61241
Fire		
Kissamos Dept	0822	24333
Forest Police of Kissamos	0822	24112
Kissamos Port Authority	0822	22024
Administration		
Kissamos Town Hall	0822	22633
Community Office, Kolymbari	0824	22110
Community Office, Platanos	0822	41337
Bus Station, Kastelli	0822	22035
Telephone Enquiries		131

Name of Service	Telephone Code	Number
Tourist Accommodation		
Kissamos District	0822	22315

Telephone Numbers and Addresses of the following are included in the booklet 'Green Tourism Guide of Kissamos Province'

SELINOS

	Telephone Code	Number
Medical		
Kandanos	28230	22550
Paleochora	28230	41211
Administration		
Municipality of Kandanos (Town Hall)	28230	22360/22367
Town Hall, Paleochora	28230	83040
Citizens Service Center		
Kandanos	28230	22366
Paleochora	28230	41751
Police		
Kandanos	28230	22100
Paleochora	28230	41111
Fire		
Kandanos	28230	22199
Paleochora	28230	22199
Bus Station		
Kandanos – Grigorakis Tavern	28230	22005
Paleochora	0821	93052/93306

APPENDIX 4
Summary of Walks

Walk	Distance (km/miles)	Time (hrs)	Grade	Start	Finish
1	5 (3¼)	1½	2	Kolimbari	Afrata
2	6 (3¾)	2	1	Afrata	Afrata
3	6 (3¾)	3–4	3/4	Afrata	Afrata
4	7.5 (4¾)	3	2	Afrata	Ravdouha
5	7 (4½)	3–4	3/4	Kato Ravdouha	Nopigia
6	5.25 (3¼)	2	1	Kastelli fishing harbour	Kastelli
7	2.63 (1¾)	2	1	Kastelli fish harbour or Mavros Molos	Mavros Molos or Kastelli
8	22 (13½)	7	3+	Kaliviani	Kaliviani
9	32 (20¼)	10	4	Kaliviani	Kaliviani
10	15 (9¼)	6–7	4	Kaliviani	Kaliviani
11	10 (6¼)	4	4	Kaliviani	Kaliviani
12	7.5 (4¾)	3½	2	Kaliviani	Kaliviani
13A	10 (6¼)	3	2	Kavoussi	Phalasarna
13B	13.5 (8½)	6	3	Kavoussi	Kaliviani
14	11.25 (7)	6	4	South of Platanos	Platanos
15	6.5 (4)	4	3	Voulgaro	Malathiros
16	8.45 (5¼)	3½	2	Topolia	Topolia
17	5.6 (3)	2½	2	Sprikari	Polyrinia
18	1.5 (1)	½–¾	1	Katsomatados	Katsomatados
19	14 (8¾)	5	3	Katsomatados	Katsomatados
20	9 (5½)	4	3	Katsomatados	Katsomatados
21	8 (5)	3½	3	Katsomatados	Katsomatados
22	9 (5½)	3½	2/3	Katsomatados	Katsomatados
23	13.6 (8½)	6	3	Katsomatados	Topolia/ Katsomatados
24	8.8 (5½)	3	3	Vlatos	Topolia
25	5.2 (3¼)	5½	3/4	Elos	Elos
26	7.6 (4¾)	3	2	Elos	Vlatos
27	7.25 (4½)	4	3	Elos	Elos
28	8 (5)	3½	3	Junction Strovles/Aligi	Sassalos

Walk	Distance (km/miles)	Time (hrs)	Grade	Start	Finish
29	3.6 (2¼)	1¼	1	Louhia	Vathi
30	9 (5½)	4½–5	3	Kefali	Kefali
31	7.5 (4¾)	3	2/2½	Vathi	Vathi
32	2 (1¼)	1½	2	Plockamiana	Plockamiana
33	12 (7½)	4½–5	3	Kefali	Kefali
34	10.5 (6½)	5	3/4	Chrisoskalitissis	Elafonisos
35	3.6 (2¼)	2	1	Paleochora ferryboat jetty	Paleochora ferryboat jetty
36	12 (7½)	4½	4	Cape Krios	Elafonisos
37	6.5 (4)	4	3	Paleochora	Paleochora
38	12 (7½)	5	3	Paleochora	Paleochora
39	5 (3)	2–2½	1	Kandanos	Kandanos
40	5 (3)	2	2	Kandanos	Kandanos
41	12 (7½)	4	2	Kandanos	Kandanos
42	14.5 (9)	6	3/4	Kandanos	Kandanos
43	22 (14)	8–9	3/4	Kandanos	Kandanos
44	6 (3¾)	2–3	1/2	Kandanos	Kandanos
45	4 (2½)	1¼	2	Kandanos	Plemeniana

CP – Car Park

Degree of Difficulty

1 – Good path, moderate ascent, no navigational problems.

2 – Distinct path, steeper ascents, longer walk.

3 – Paths rough in places, ascent 610m/2000ft, exposed in places.

4 – Wild walking, ascent 722m/2400ft plus, exposed, compass needed.

NOTES

NOTES

NOTES

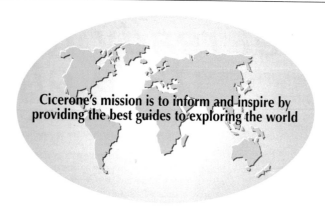

Cicerone's mission is to inform and inspire by providing the best guides to exploring the world

Since its foundation over 30 years ago, Cicerone has specialised in publishing guidebooks and has built a reputation for quality and reliability. It now publishes nearly 300 guides to the major destinations for outdoor enthusiasts, including Europe, UK and the rest of the world.

Written by leading and committed specialists, Cicerone guides are recognised as the most authoritative. They are full of information, maps and illustrations so that the user can plan and complete a successful and safe trip or expedition – be it a long face climb, a walk over Lakeland fells, an alpine traverse, a Himalayan trek or a ramble in the countryside.

With a thorough introduction to assist planning, clear diagrams, maps and colour photographs to illustrate the terrain and route, and accurate and detailed text, Cicerone guides are designed for ease of use and access to the information.

If the facts on the ground change, or there is any aspect of a guide that you think we can improve, we are always delighted to hear from you.

Cicerone Press
2 Police Square Milnthorpe Cumbria LA7 7PY
Tel:01539 562 069   Fax:01539 563 417
e-mail:info@cicerone.co.uk   web:www.cicerone.co.uk

CICERONE